CW00344710

# Women As Bishops

# Women As Bishops

Edited by

James Rigney
with Mark D. Chapman

mowbray

Published by Mowbray
*A Continuum Imprint*
The Tower Building
11 York Road
London SE1 7NX

80 Maiden Lane, Suite 704
New York
NY 10038

www.continuumbooks.com

All rights reserved. No part of this publication may be reproduced or transmitted in any form or by any means, electronic or mechanical, including photocopying, recording or any information storage or retrieval system, without permission in writing from the publishers.

Copyright © James Rigney and contributors, 2008

First published 2008

British Library Cataloguing-in-Publication Data
A catalogue record for this book is available from the British Library

Typeset by Mark D. Chapman
Printed and bound in Great Britain by Athenaeum Press Ltd, Gateshead, Tyne and Wear

ISBN 10: 0–567-03224–8
ISBN 13: 978–0-567–03224-9

# Contents

v

# Foreword by the Series Editor

This collection of essays and documents addresses the question of the ordination or consecration of women bishops in the Church of England. Some of the essays were originally presented as papers at a symposium held on a cold day at St Matthew's Church, Westminster, in March 2006. These were published in a special edition of the *Affirming Catholicism Journal* later that year. All the chapters in the present volume have been revised and updated. The chapter by David Stancliffe and Tom Wright is new to this volume, as is my epilogue, and the final three documents. Thanks are due to Thomas Kraft of Continuum for supporting the project from the outset, and also to Lisa Martell, administrator of Affirming Catholicism for organizing the symposium. A special debt of gratitude is owed to the Revd Richard Jenkins, who soon finishes his period as director of Affirming Catholicism. His contribution to the organization has been immense and his energy and dynamism will be greatly missed. It seems fitting to dedicate this volume to him as a parting gift.

Mark D. Chapman
The Feast of St Hilda, 19 November 2007

# Notes on Contributors

**Angela Berlis** is Professor of Old Catholic Church Structures at the University of Utrecht and Principal of the Old Catholic Seminary in Utrecht. She is a member of the International Roman Catholic–Old Catholic Dialogue Commission (IRAD) and Co-secretary of the Anglican–Old Catholic International Co-ordinating Council (AOCICC). She serves as a non-stipendiary priest in the Old Catholic Church.

**David Carter** is a Methodist theologian and the author of *Love Bade Me Welcome – A British Methodist Perspective on the Church*.

**Mark Chapman** is Vice-Principal of Ripon College Cuddesdon, Oxford. He has published widely in the fields of doctrine and church history.

**Charlotte Methuen** is Departmental Lecturer in Ecclesiastical History in the University of Oxford and Canon Theologian of Gloucester Cathedral. She is a member of the Anglican–Lutheran International Commission, the Faith and Order Advisory Group of the Church of England and an observer on the Meissen Commission.

**Barry Norris** is Chair of Affirming Catholicism and Vicar of Tadley St Mary in the Diocese of Winchester.

**James Rigney** is Chaplain and Director of Studies in Theology at Magdalene College, Cambridge.

**Jane Shaw** is Dean of Divinity, Chaplain and Fellow of New College, Oxford.

**David Stancliffe** is Bishop of Salisbury and president of Affirming Catholicism.

**John Wijngaards** holds a doctorate in dogmatic theology from the Gregorian University in Rome and a Licenciate of Sacred Scripture from the Pontifical Biblical Institute. As well as teaching in major seminaries, he was for ten years a lecturer of the Missionary Institute, London, which is affiliated to Middlesex University, and Louvain University. He is the author of many books, popular and academic, including three on the ordination of women.

**Tom Wright** is one of Britain's leading New Testament scholars and Bishop of Durham.

*For Richard Jenkins*
*in gratitude for his service to*
*Affirming Catholicism*

# Introduction

JAMES RIGNEY

Hastings Rashdall, sometime Dean of Carlisle and one of the foremost English 'modernist' theologians, famously wrote that 'if you believed in episcopacy it did not matter what else you disbelieved in the Church of England'. The continuing debate on the ordination of women to the episcopate draws attention to crucial matters of Anglican identity. The majority of chapters presented in this collection were originally written for, or in consequence of, a symposium organized by Affirming Catholicism and held at St Matthew's Church, Westminster, on 11 March 2006. The aim of that symposium was to enunciate a progressive Catholic position in favour of the ordination of women to the episcopate.

This collection joins an ongoing debate which has taken place not only in the General Synod of the Church of England but also in print in the years since the publication of *Women Bishops in the Church of England? A Report of the House of Bishops' Working Party on Women and the Episcopate* (London: Church House Publishing, 2004). *Women and the Episcopate* continues the discussion contained in *The Call for Women Bishops*, edited by Harriet Harris and Jane Shaw (London: SPCK, 2004) and seeks to engage critically with *Consecrated Women? A Contribution to the Women Bishops Debate*, edited by Jonathan Baker (Norwich: Canterbury Press, 2004).

Affirming Catholicism continues to believe that it is vital to redirect the debate on women and the episcopate as it is being undertaken in the Church of England. This redirection is necessary because the debate has been displaced from focusing on the rightness and timeliness of the ordination of women to the episcopate towards a discussion of how to accommodate and compensate those who say they cannot accept such a decision. While love and courtesy make the second of those issues an important one to consider, it nevertheless constitutes part only of

1

the debate; it is a secondary part when compared to the process of discernment and decision that is called for by the fundamental issue.

Is the ordination of women to the episcopate possible and desirable? If it is possible and desirable is this the right time for the Church of England to proceed to such a decision? The authors of these essays offer an affirmative answer to both of these questions and, in the papers that follow, present the theological grounds on which that affirmation rests.

The first two chapters in this collection, by Barry Norris and Charlotte Methuen, question the issues of validity and competence which have been enrolled to forestall progress towards admitting women into the threefold ministry in the Church of England. The Church of England, as a reforming branch of the Catholic Church claims the right to carry out reforms and changes that enhance and affirm its life and witness in accordance with the Catholic faith as we have received it without thereby breaking essential principles of apostolic faith and practice. We do not see that this compromises our apostolic calling. Instead it gives focus and urgency to our continuing mission within the universal Church to proclaim afresh the gospel in each generation.

Another strand of argument put forward against the ordination of women to the episcopate rests on the alleged damage such a move would do to the Church of England's ecumenical relations. John Wijngaards' paper powerfully discloses and discusses the diversity of theological opinion within the Roman Catholic Church in relation to the ordination of women, and gives voice to a substantial body of theological opinion which is often silenced beneath the weight of centralized Church pronouncements. The Bishop of Salisbury, David Stancliffe, and the Bishop of Durham, Tom Wright, continue the discussion of this issue in the light of the address by Cardinal Walter Kasper, President of the Pontifical Council for Promoting Christian Unity, to the Church of England House of Bishops meeting in June 2006. Their essay was originally published by *Fulcrum*, and we are grateful to its authors, and the editor, Canon Graham Kings, for allowing its reproduction here.

In a debate where the opponents of the ordination of women often present ecumenical issues in a light which prioritizes the Roman Catholic tradition over all other churches with which the Church of England has ecumenical relations it is important to hear from those other partners. David Carter and Angela Berlis offer contributions from the Methodist and Old Catholic traditions respectively. Both chapters disclose a long and valuable engagement with questions about the nature of episcopacy, and encourage the Church of England to learn from those with whom it has established covenant relationships or is indeed already in full communion, including mutual recognition of ministries. The papers of the Orthodox/Old Catholic colloquium which appeared in the *Anglican Theological Review* in the summer of 2002 indicate that even within Orthodoxy – another tradition cited as a potential ecumenical casualty if the Church of England were to continue to ordain women – there are theologians whose understanding of the Chalcedonian definition of the Incarnation makes them look at the possibility of the ordination of women in a new and favourable light.

The Church exists in time and is a unit for measuring time. Consequently throughout this collection we offer some historical perspectives on the Church's understanding of ministry in general and episcopacy in particular. Charlotte Methuen's 'Women with Oversight' examines evidence from the Early Church concerned with the roles played by women in ecclesial communities. While opponents of women's ordination frequently allege that such a move is driven by a secular feminist agenda against which the Church is required to stand in the security of its tradition, it is valuable to be reminded of the pragmatic reasons by which the male episcopate took the ascendancy, conforming to a leadership structure derived from, and acceptable to, secular institutions. Yet Methuen's chapter also offers inspiring glimpses of a fuller participation by women in the orders of ministry as they emerged in the Early Church. However, if the evidence does not

3

unequivocally demonstrate that women shared the ministry of the episcope, neither does it show categorically that they did not. To those who believe that the Church must spend more time 'mining the mind of the Fathers' before settling the issue, Methuen's chapter shows that such investigations will be inconclusive and that in fact the issue is one that must be settled within our own time and within our contemporary church polity.

Mark Chapman's analysis of the dispute over the Jerusalem bishopric in 1841 draws attention to the specific historic circumstances in which 'the Catholic doctrine of episcopacy' arose in Anglicanism. He also indicates the manner in which the emphasis placed on one view of episcopacy because of particular historic conditions leads to the disregard of other aspects of episcopacy, such as its corporate character. The historical contingencies that lie behind universalized models of doctrine and church order is something which it is crucial to keep in mind.

The question of the ordination of women (to whatever order of ministry) remains an open and disputed issue – as does the ordination of practising homosexuals. The aim should be to remain within the same church in as great a degree of communion as possible ... whatever one's view on these disputed and yet to be resolved matters. The debate over the ordination of women to the episcopate requires the Anglican Church to ask itself what it understands by bishops. We are challenged to ensure that our understanding is one that will be of service to the Church and not merely a structure for defensiveness and discrimination.

The most recent figures on the deployment of women in the Church of England reveal that the number of women clergy in the Church of England has risen to an average of 25.8 per cent of all diocesan clergy. Women now account for 17 per cent of full-time stipendiary clergy in the dioceses and 8 per cent of senior posts, including deans, archdeacons, other cathedral clergy and area deans. Although the legal obstacles to appointing women bishops are now on the verge of disappearing, the fierce opposition to the ordination of women priests continues. Jonathan Sedgwick's *Why Women Priests? The Ordination of Women and the Apostolic Ministry* was among the first publications issued under the auspices of Affirming Catholicism. In an earlier version of this book, which was produced as a special edition of the *Affirming Catholicism Journal* (2006), this booklet was republished with only minimal alteration. Yet, while some of the issues raised by Sedgwick are still not settled, the Church has moved on. It is 30 years since the General Synod of the Church of England agreed that there was 'no fundamental objection to the ordination of women to the priesthood'. There are now over 2,500 women clergy and for the past three years there have been equal numbers of men and women in training for ordained ministry.

Opposition to the ordination of women as bishops has the potential to do violence to the doctrine of the Incarnation which lies at the heart of our experience and identity as Christians. As the spirit-filled body of Christ the reception of developments within the apostolic faith is a mark of its ecclesiological vitality. Growing into the wholeness which the Incarnation invites us to do involves focusing on God in his fullness in a manner that is released from any consideration of gender particularity. The Church cannot be true to its calling if it legislates to restrict its experience of the fullness of God.

# 1

## The Calling of Women as Bishops

JANE SHAW

### Calling

On the morning of her ordination to the diaconate, Carolyn Tanner Irish explained to her young son why she would be ordained a second time a few months later, talking to him about the nature of the threefold ordained ministry. He went away and thought about it for a few minutes, and then came back and asked, 'Hey Mom, how come you decided not to be a bishop?' The punchline is that she did become a bishop, the Bishop of Utah, in the Episcopal Church in America. Harriet Harris and I decided to open the book we recently edited on women bishops, *The Call for Women Bishops*,[1] with that story because we did not want to lose sight of the sense that both women and men are called to particular offices in the Church. They are called out from their communities, on the basis of their gifts, their spiritual depth and their inner stability. It is the call with which we must begin: the godly call. This is important to state from the outset because we have got ourselves into a topsy-turvy situation in the Church of England in which our starting-point has instead become: what shall we do for the opponents of women bishops? Our starting-point should, rather, be the call to women and men to exercise the ministry of oversight within the Church. This emerges from the most fundamental of all starting-points – our theological anthropology: namely, that men and women are made in the image and likeness of God.

---

1   Harriet Harris and Jane Shaw (eds), *The Call for Women Bishops* (London: SPCK, 2004), p. 3.

There is, of course, a delicate balance between the divine call and our capacity, as humans, to discern that call within the context of the earthly Church. Critics of women in ordained ministry frequently say that in ordaining women, the Church is just following society and bowing to secular pressure. In making that charge, those critics fail to recognize the supernatural element of the call that women, and the communities in which they exercise their ministry, experience. In fact, the Church falls prey to its own temptations and secularizing pressures, not least the sin of misogyny. This was a recurring theme in the essays in *The Call for Women Bishops* from contributors all around the Anglican Communion: England, North America, Africa, and New Zealand. Even when we say that there is a will for the ordination and consecration of women as bishops to go forward, even when we say there are no theological objections, we stumble and hesitate and stall. Why? What stops the Church from proceeding clearly?

## What stops the church from proceeding?

First, there are cultural factors to do with the perception of women's and men's roles. We have allowed 'gut-level' stuff to interfere with our theology. As Walter Makhulu, the former Archbishop of Central Africa, starkly puts it: 'Sadly, patriarchy reigns supreme and, in central Africa, men in the Church have tended to use the culture to maintain their attitude to women.'[2] Some parts of the Anglican Communion, for instance, parts of Africa, have passed legislation allowing women into all three orders of ministry, but women have not actually been promoted. Other provinces, including England and Australia, have stalled on allowing women into the episcopate. We have allowed our cultural attitudes about leadership and gender to affect (perhaps infect?) our theology. We have thus created a 'stained-glass' ceiling. For example, we have blithely assumed that women –

---

2    Harris and Shaw, *The Call for Women Bishops*, p. 34.

ordained as priests in the Church of England only in the last decade – do not have the experience to be bishops, all the time ignoring the ways in which they may have exercised leadership, and indeed oversight, in their jobs as company directors or headmistresses of schools before ordination. This has been given as a reason to stall on women bishops: it is said that there are not enough women 'with the experience' to be bishops. The truth is that we have ignored women's invaluable experience, and if we continue to do this we will lose their gifts of leadership. This brings me to theological ideas about leadership.

Secondly, what theological presuppositions about leadership have hampered the Church's path to clarity on the issue of women bishops? At the Anglo-Catholic end of the Church, some have placed too much weight on Christ's maleness, and this is related to other issues. If we see the priest purely as an icon of Christ, we might not only mistakenly associate priesthood with maleness but we might also unhelpfully emphasize christology over trinitarian theology. As Lucy Winkett has put it: how might a theology of the trinity help us think in a more relational way about leadership, not least at an episcopal level?[3]

Thirdly, we have used vague and muddy perceptions of what is going on, on the ground – in the parishes, in the wider Church – as an excuse for not proceeding with the admission of women to the episcopate. In fact, very little proper sociological research has been done to assess the impact of women's ordained ministry in the Church, with the exception of Ian Jones' useful but by no means comprehensive report, *Women and Priesthood in the Church of England: Ten Years on.*[4] We rely on hearsay and anecdote, and too easily give into rumours and fears of splits. To put it another way: how has the debate on women bishops been affected by the perceptions rather than the realities of what is going on, on the ground? If we proceed with women bishops on the lines of the

---

3   Author's conversation with Lucy Winkett.
4   Ian Jones, *Women and Priesthood in the Church of England: Ten Years On* (London: Church House Publishing, 2004).

recent TEA (Transferred Episcopal Arrangements) proposal in the Church of England, then the question will become this: how will those perceptions, rather than realities, affect, inform and even dictate what the national church does?

This all relates to my fourth point, which is this: to what extent does fear affect what we do and how we do it: fear of the unknown; fear of splitting the Church; fear of offending one's friends? This fear has led already to two deeply un-Catholic things: the splitting of the threefold order of ministry (that is, the integrity of Anglican orders has been broken in the way the Church of England proceeded with the ordination of women first only as deacons; and then only as deacons and priests), and the Act of Synod. The Act of Synod was intended to provide provincial episcopal oversight, but it has in effect provided alternative episcopal oversight. It has opened an ecclesiological can of worms, such that people now feel they have a right to have a bishop of their choice if they do not like their bishop's views on x, y or z; this has become particularly acute in the debate about homosexuality, and we have probably seen only the tip of the iceberg of the proliferation of this sort of alternative oversight. The Act of Synod was a compromise measure, intended to hold the Church together. Transferred Episcopal Arrangements are meant to be the same thing. The irony is that such compromise measures are actually doing the opposite of the holding the Church together; they are leading to its fracturing. What price, then, supposed 'unity'?

Fifthly, we constantly use 'bad' understandings of scripture and tradition in our debates about women bishops; that is, we abandon critical scholarship for crude interpretations of scripture and for an understanding of tradition that makes it frozen in a particular time rather than dynamic. The Holy Spirit is leading us on, but we stop up our eyes and ears to that divine movement.

Finally, in ecumenical considerations about this question, the tendency is to look only to Rome rather than to the Protestant churches with whom we have or are building relations. These include the churches of the Porvoo Agreement (such as the

Evangelical–Lutheran Churches of Norway, Finland and the Church of Sweden). The most obvious case here is that in the talks between the Methodist Church and Church of England, our not having women in the episcopate has been a real stumbling block for the Methodists.

These six factors – and probably many more too – leave us with a muddled approach; we are oriented towards the question of women bishops from the wrong angle, so to speak. In the Church of England we will get women bishops some time in the next decade – that seems fairly certain now – but the question is how, and at what cost? Instead of a single-clause measure, which would recognize the equal standing of women and men in the eyes of God, retain the integrity of our ecclesiology and our theology, and enable fair and just employment within the Church, we have the possibility of a measure strapped by compromise. This attitude of compromise pervades both the Rochester and Guildford Reports, the two recent results of working parties on the ordination and consecration of women as bishops in the Church of England. Those reports and the attitude of compromise within them throw up two practical problems which I wish to discuss briefly before concluding this chapter.

## Two practical problems

First, much is made of collegiality in both of these reports, especially the Guildford Report, but it is all directed towards male colleagues who are opposed to women as bishops, and towards making those men comfortable. No thought has been given to the conditions under which women will become bishops and will exercise oversight. How will they enter the 'male club' that is the House of Bishops? Will they have to wear bullet-proof vests to their consecration as Barbara Harris – the first woman to be consecrated a bishop in the Anglican Communion – did? How can we overcome the sense of isolation that any woman as a bishop will face in the Church of England? My suggestion would be that from the outset we appoint more than one female bishop.

We should have three or four women appointed as bishops right from the start. This is possible given that bishops are appointed by the crown rather than elected.[5] This would avoid both tokenism and isolation.

Secondly, why is the Church of England acting as if no one has done this before? It is partly, I suppose, a result of our sometimes rather isolated and superior attitude, compounded by our inward-looking perspective which undermines much of our sense of mission, but it also reveals that little or no validity is given to women's experiences of exercising authority within other churches, even our sister Anglican churches. Those compiling the Rochester and Guildford Reports have not attempted to communicate with or learn from female bishops in USA, Canada and New Zealand about their experiences of being bishops, nor the people in the dioceses in which they have served; nor has any thought been given to finding out how women in other Protestant denominations – Methodist, Baptist – have experienced the exercise of oversight. The Rochester Report consulted one female bishop, briefly.[6] The Guildford Report declared that the working party 'did meet separately with the Archbishop of Canterbury ... its chairman engaged with the House's theological group and the PEVs, and individual members engaged informally with diocesan colleagues and others'.[7] There is no evidence that this working party, which produced the compromise TEA solution, met with

---

5  Since the writing of this chapter, the new Prime Minister, Gordon Brown, has questioned the Crown Appointments System, but bishops will still be appointed, rather than elected, and therefore the co-ordination of appointing several women as bishops at the same time remains possible in the Church of England.

6  *Women Bishops in the Church of England? A Report of the House of Bishops' Working Party on Women in the Episcopate* (London: Church House Publishing, 2004). This information is based on the author's conversations with some members of the working party and supporting secretariat as to whether female bishops were consulted.

7  *Women in the Episcopate: The Guildford Group Report* (London: Church House Publishing, 2006), pp. 3–4.

any women, ordained or otherwise, and the working party had only one female member. This seems to suggest that the report was written wholly with the Provincial Episcopal Visitors (Flying Bishops) and opponents in mind. This brings me back to one of my first points: that we have got our starting-point wrong. Instead of saying, 'Let's have women bishops', we constantly start with the question: what shall we do for the opponents?

The working parties that produced the Guildford and Rochester reports missed the opportunity to learn from the practical experiences of female bishops, including how diocesan women bishops dealt with opposition and were received in their dioceses. For example, the Bishop of Rhode Island, Geralyn Wolf, has found informal but totally workable schemes for working with those parishes that were opposed to her episcopal ministry; she has valuable insights to offer, but no one in the Church of England has officially asked her for them. Furthermore, if the Church of England wanted to make the reception of women as bishops easier, it could have done so – partly by listening to the experiences of women bishops in other parts of the Communion – but it does not seem to have the will.

## Conclusion

The Church of England has approached the question of women bishops in a muddled way, seeking to appease the small minority of opponents rather than proceeding with integrity and clarity. A single-clause measure for women bishops is the only principled course of action. It is the only option that is true to the Church's own theology of human nature: that humankind is made in the image and likeness of God. As Barbara Harris put it of her own episcopal ministry in the diocese of Massachusetts: 'Women and girls were encouraged to feel that they truly had a place in the church and people of colour expressed their pride and their joy in

God's doing a new thing.'[8] Or as Jane Holmes Dixon, retired suffragan bishop of Washington DC, put it: 'There is nothing – no thing – that speaks of God like seeing someone like you in that sacred space.'[9]

---

8    Barbara C. Harris, 'Living the Change: On Being the First Woman Bishop in the Anglican Communion', in Harris and Shaw, *The Call for Women Bishops,* p. 29

9    Sermon preached at the service held in Christ Church Cathedral, Oxford, to celebrate the tenth anniversary of the ordination of women as priests in the Church of England, April 2004.

# 2

## *The Concept of Validity*

BARRY NORRIS

> If we trace back the power of ordination from hand to
> hand of course we shall come to the apostles at last – we
> know we do, as a plain historical fact. (J. H. Newman,
> *Thoughts on the Ministerial Commission*, 1833)

Newman wrote his summary of apostolic succession with a fine
disregard of the historical problems involved. His concern was not
primarily the natural succession of bishops, but the very basis of
the Church, which was, as he saw it, being undermined by the
state. Apostolic succession, he believed, establishes and
guarantees that basis. Its sign is the succession in office of bishops.
Only bishops in the apostolic succession can validly ordain. In the
current debate it is therefore important to consider the two
notions of apostolic succession and validity.

### Apostolic succession

In the past decades there has been considerable ecumenical
convergence in the understanding of apostolicity and apostolic
succession, particularly in the work leading to the agreements of
Meissen, Porvoo and Reuilly and in the ARCIC discussions.
Apostolicity and apostolic succession are now understood to be
the work of the whole Church in its faithfulness to the witness of
Jesus Christ. In other words, the entire Christian community
maintains this faithfulness to the apostolic faith and transmits it
from one generation to the next. The disputed area is the precise
relationship between succession in this broad sense and the
particular sense, which concerns the place of the episcopate as a
sign of that succession.

The various 'agreed statements' of multilateral and bilateral dialogues all start from a point where churches which have episcopacy can now acknowledge a continuity in apostolic faith in those churches which do not have the historic episcopate, and churches like our own are ready to acknowledge that episcopacy is not an *absolute* guarantee of the apostolicity of the Church. This means that the past situation of mutual disavowals is over. The way forward is opening up for a mutual recognition of ministries in which no side need deny its past but rather may look to a fuller expression of apostolicity in a united church.

It is worth noting in the context of the ordination of women to the presbyterate and episcopate, that in the Elucidations of the 1979 *ARCIC Final Report* it seems that the Roman Catholic Church would not be prevented from acknowledging the 'validity' of the ministry of the Anglican Church simply by reason of the fact that women are ordained.

> The Commission believes that the principles upon which its doctrinal agreement rests are not affected by such ordinations; for it was concerned with the origin and nature of the ordained ministry and not with the question who can or who cannot be ordained. Objections, however substantial, to the ordination of women are of a different kind from objections raised in the past against the validity of Anglican Orders in general.[1]

The Reformed–Roman Catholic dialogue in the United States, *Ministry in the Church*, states:

> Because of the growing consensus among Reformed and Roman Catholic theologians that there is no insurmountable biblical or dogmatic obstacle to the ordination of women and because of the needs of the

---

1    *ARCIC Final Report: Windsor 1979* (London: SPCK, 1981), p. 44.

people of God. ... we conclude that the ordination of
women must be part of the church's life.[2]

The same is true of the work of the Lutheran–Roman Catholic
international conversations. The WCC text on this matter
concludes: 'Openness to each other holds out the possibility that
the Spirit will speak to one Church through the insights of
another.'[3]

No one Church can claim to be the *exclusive* repository of
apostolicity guaranteed through episcopal laying-on of hands
historically traceable back to the Apostles. It is notable that the
Roman Catholic Bishops' statement in response to the Rochester
Report takes a step back from the ecumenical consensus of many
years' standing to a more conservative, narrow and scholastic
view of apostolic succession and its allied concept of validity and
sacramental character. I now turn to these latter notions.

**Validity**

Validity is essentially a juridical term applied to a sacrament, to
determine that the divinely appointed sign has been duly
performed and to which therefore is necessarily attached the
divinely promised gift. This concept plays an important part in the
discussions about the sacraments, particularly in relation to holy
order. For a sacrament to be valid, a validly ordained minister
must administer that sacrament. A validly ordained minister is
one ordained by a bishop standing in the apostolic succession.

Historically the issues were further complicated and un-
necessarily narrowed in the Middle Ages by scholastic debate
which led to an emphasis on the laying-on of hands as a causal
process 'producing' mechanistically sacramental grace and

2   *Ministry in the Church: a statement by the Theology Section of the Roman
    Catholic/Presbyterian–Reformed Consultation* (Richmond, VA: no
    publisher, 1971), p. 13.
3   *Scripture, Tradition and Traditions: The Fourth World Conference on Faith
    and Order* (Montreal: WCC, 1963).

sacramental effect or 'character'. (In referring to 'scholasticism' I mean both that of the medieval schools, and also neo-scholasticism as taught in Roman Catholic seminaries and universities.)

The notion of 'sacramental character' is itself a difficult one, related to sacramental grace. Sacramental character, as a sort of ontological effect produced in the soul of the ordained, is a difficult concept for non-scholastics and many Church of England folk. On this, Fr Piet Fransen remarks that 'the tendency to enhance sacramental character has produced a sort of complex metaphysical superstructure due to a very jejune theology of grace'.[4] Augustine certainly limited it to the external rite, the visible and audible expression of the faith of the Church, and its inviolability consisting of the fact of the ordinand being adopted into his or her '*ordo*' of the Church's ministry.

Thomas Aquinas follows this line, but early scholasticism showed a tendency to include in the description of the character the ontological effect of ordination (legitimate membership of the college of ministers) as well as the simple rite, which hitherto had 'characterized' the ordinand. Aquinas resisted this and stuck to the principle that ordination places the ordinand *in the face of the community* in the name of Christ. Subsequent scholastic theology, ignoring Aquinas, translated all this into baldly ontological terms. Put simply, ordination by a bishop in the apostolic succession gives 'something' to the ordinand: i.e. the transmission of *potestas* with or without a bestowal of a certain charisma. Grace is objectified and reified, and can be possessed by an individual and transmitted. But it also leaves the community out of the equation. If this is all cause and effect, a break in the chain would influence the outcome.

However, in over-emphasizing the ontological many theologians are standing against their own tradition, and would do well to heed Fr Fransen's words:

4    Piet Fransen in Karl Rahner (ed.), *Encyclopaedia of Theology* (London: Burns & Oates, 1975), p. 1146.

We believe that the more realistic notion of the character as held in ancient times should be taken up again. ... this incorporation into the college of his [*sic*] 'order' implies a number of rights and duties. Its principal element is the mission of service with regard to the community of the Church and of all humankind. ... this aspect of the character may be based on the fidelity of the divine election rather than on an ontological quality taken separately.[5]

## An alternative approach deriving from the Orthodox tradition

The concept of validity is very much part of scholastic and neo-scholastic theology. I want now to present an alternative way of thinking about Holy Order from the Orthodox perspective and the personalist philosophy expounded by John Zizioulas, particularly in *Being as Communion*.[6] Zizioulas' general view is that any theology of ministry must have a pneumatological foundation, as well as a christological one, as is particularly emphasized in scholasticism. In this pneumatological context all ministries are identical with Christ's ministry, not parallel to it; all categories of separation are transcended, and ministry can only be understood within the community.

Zizioulas is emphatic that no ministry can stand outside or above the community. This approach completely confounds scholastic causal thinking and the ontological view, but also a functional understanding of ministry in terms of delegation from the community to the ordained. Ordination to the ministry within the eucharistic community carries the implication that the gift of the Holy Spirit cannot exist outside the ordained person's relationship to the ecclesial community. Zizioulas thus rejects

---

5    Rahner, *Encyclopaedia of Theology*, p.1147.
6    John Zizioulas, *Being as Communion* (London: Darton, Longman & Todd, 1985).

both the 'catholic' and the Protestant view of ministry, for both
these views are rooted in the notion of causality, which has its
immediate origins in scholastic Aristotelianism. Without the
notion of 'relationship' the ministry loses its character both as a
charisma of the Spirit, part of the *koinonia*, and as service
(*diakonia*). Ministry renders the Church as a relational reality, a
mystery of love. One cannot possess anything as an individual
within this realm of love. It is equally invidious to say that
someone in a state of love simply 'functions'. Love has its own
dynamic and rationale which cuts a swathe through the
individualistic ontology described earlier.

When Zizioulas turns to the question of 'validity' of ministry he
has some important observations to make.[7] He asserts that
'validity' is essentially a juridical term and implies that the
ministry can be isolated from the rest of ecclesiology. 'Validity' is
then judged by certain 'objective' criteria, ignoring the point that
these criteria were originally integral and organic parts of the
concrete eucharistic community and make no sense apart from
their context in the community.

So by looking at a community first, and then at the criteria, it
becomes clear that 'the recognition of ministries becomes in fact a
recognition of communities in an existential sense' and that
furthermore, 'this means that a difference in ministerial form as
such cannot determine the recognition of a ministry'.[8] This seems
to offer a way forward ecumenically. Zizioulas suggests that it
should now be possible for divided communities to recognize
each other as communities relating to God and the world through
their ministries rather than by recognizing each other's 'orders'.

With reference to apostolicity, the entire notion becomes
eschatologized; the apostles cannot be enclosed in the past.
Apostolicity is best defined not in terms of historical perspectives
but in terms of the Church listening to her own voice, which
comes from her eschatological nature as a 'sign' of a redeemed

---

7  Zizioulas, *Being as Communion*, pp. 243ff.
8  Zizioulas, *Being as Communion*, p. 244.

creation. In this context we can understand Jürgen Moltmann's preference to speak not of apostolic succession but of the 'church's apostolic procession to the end of time'.[9]

## Conclusion

The Canons of the Church of England (especially section 4) assert the provincial autonomy of that church within the universal Church. In particular, Canon A4 maintains the competence of the Church of England to order its ordained ministry so that all those lawfully ordained may be accounted as within the apostolic ministry. In other words, if the Church of England decides synodically that women may be ordained into the threefold ministry, and this decision is ratified by parliament, they will lawfully be so ordained.

This effectively cuts away the ground from the opponents of women's ordination who argue from the position of the invalidity of such ordinations by appealing to a higher authority – that of the Roman Catholic Church – whose jurisdiction the Church of England repudiated at the Reformation.

But, as has been demonstrated in this chapter, this approach would not work unless it were conceived within a narrow and outmoded theological model of apostolic succession, sacramental character, and validity, which many Roman Catholic theologians no longer hold. There is undoubtedly now a more helpful and constructive theological consensus on these matters which has superseded these older models.

Such an appeal to conservative theological arguments within Roman Catholicism would appear to be a desperate clutching at theological straws and is totally at odds with much contemporary Roman Catholic theology and the Anglican theological tradition and polity. Within that tradition and polity, the body of believers may have absolute assurance in the ordained ministry of the Church of England: a ministry of women and men.

---

9   Jürgen Moltmann, *The Church in the Power of the Spirit* (London: SCM Press, 1977), p. 321.

# 3

## 'To Visit, Repress, Redress, Reform, Correct, Restrain and Amend': Historical Reflections on the Competence of the Church of England

CHARLOTTE METHUEN

The question of the competence of the Church of England to make decisions – which is one of the foundation stones of the arguments against the ordination of women – is one which has long exercised the minds of its bishops and theologians. This chapter considers the Church of England's understanding of itself as a church and the competencies which it takes on as a consequence.

The Church of England took on its distinctive form as a national church in 1534 when King Henry VIII was declared by act of parliament to be 'Supreme Head of the Church of England called the *Anglicana Ecclesia*', and charged to 'visit, repress, redress, reform, order, correct restrain and amend all such error, heresies, abuses offences, contempts and enormities' as might exist in that Church,

> to the pleasure of Almighty God, the increase of virtue in Christian religion and for the conservation of the peace, unity and tranquillity of this realm; any usage, custom, foreign laws, foreign authority, prescription, or any other thing or things to the contrary hereof notwithstanding.[1]

---

1    Act of Supremacy 1534, in Gerald Bray (ed.), *Documents of the English Reformation* (Cambridge: John Clarke, 1994), pp. 113–14.

In so declaring, Henry and his ministers stood in the tradition of princes who felt themselves responsible for the proper faith of their people – an important motivation for a good number of princes of that era. Indeed, the sixteenth century saw different political arrangements in different parts of Europe giving rise to churches with different characters and competences, some of which continued to look to Rome whilst others did not. Even in those areas which continued to regard the pope as the nominal head of the Church, the monarch might have many of the powers held in England by the king. In France, the Concordat of Bologna (1509) devolved to the king the power to appoint bishops and to collect monastic revenues. In the Spanish kingdoms, the Church and its instrument, the Inquisition, were firmly under the control of the king and queen. The political powers and financial advantage to the monarchs in Spain and France were much what they were to Henry VIII in England, and the French Church manifested its national character through a distinct reluctance to implement the decisions of the Council of Trent, which it ignored until after 1615, and even then, 'the monarchy would only recognise the doctrinal sections'.[2] The concept of the national church became more developed after the Reformation, and shaped not only the more obviously national Protestant churches, but also the national manifestations of the Roman Catholic Church.

The challenge to the national churches of the sixteenth century, whether or not they looked to Rome, was to determine what it meant to be the true Church of Christ in any particular realm. This depended on the definition of 'true Church of Christ'. In England, the response to this challenge followed the definition of the Church found in the Augsburg Confession (1530), which proclaimed 'The Church is the congregation of saints, in which the Gospel is rightly taught and the Sacraments are rightly administered' (Article VII). This was definitive for Lutheran

---

2    Diarmaid MacCulloch, *Reformation: Europe's House Divided 1490–1700* (London: Allen Lane, 2003), p. 474.

churches, and very important, too, for Calvinists. Henry VIII's 'King's Book' noted a tendency to assume that the term 'church' referred to the 'the place wherein the word of God is commonly preached and the sacraments ministered and used', rather than understanding the Church to be the community of those who receive teaching and sacraments in faith.[3] Since God calls people

> without exception of persons or privilege of place; therefore this holy church is also catholic, that is to say, not limited to any one place or region of the world, but is in every place universally through the world, where it pleaseth God to call people to him in the profession of Christ's name and faith, be it in Europe, Afric [*sic*], or Asia.[4]

These churches have different forms of government, but are all part of the catholic Church, 'relieved, nourished, and fortified by his holy and invincible word and his sacraments, which in all places have each of them their own proper force and strength'.[5] The unity of the Church is conserved, not by the 'bishop of Rome's authority or doctrine', but by the Holy Spirit and the preservation of apostolic doctrine; this unity 'is not divided by distance of place nor by diversity of traditions and ceremonies'.[6] As a consequence of this understanding of the catholicity of the Church, the King's Book can maintain: 'Every Christian man ought to honour, give credence, and to follow the particular church or that region so ordered ... wherein he is born or inhabiteth.'[7]

---

3   *The King's Book or a Necessary Doctrine and Erudition for any Christian Man, 1543* (London: SPCK, 1932), p. 32.
4   *The King's Book*, p. 33.
5   *The King's Book*, p. 33.
6   *The King's Book*, p. 34.
7   *The King's Book*, p. 36.

Under Elizabeth I, the definition of the Church found in the *Confessio Augustana* became bound up with a focus on discipline commonly found in Calvinist churches: Article 3 of the Eleven Articles (1559) acknowledged 'that Church to be the spouse of Christ, wherein the Word of God is truly taught, the sacraments orderly administered according to Christ's institution, and the authority of the keys duly used'.[8] A similar definition of the Church, based on word and sacrament, can be found also in Article 19 of the Thirty-nine Articles:

> The visible Church of Christ is a congregation of faithful men, in the which the pure Word of God is preached, and the Sacraments be duly ministered according to Christ's ordinance in all those things that of necessity are requisite to the same.

The Eleven Articles make an explicit distinction between the wider Church, as defined by word, sacrament and the use of the keys, and 'particular churches', of which the Eleven Articles maintained 'that every such particular church hath authority to institute, to change, to clean put away ceremonies and other ecclesiastical rites, as they be superfluous, or be absurd, and to constitute other making more to seemliness, to order or to edification'.[9] Particular churches might make their own decisions about ceremonies and ecclesiastical rites, although the articles beg the central question of which rites and customs might be deemed absurd and superfluous, and what brings seemliness, order and edification.

Article 20 of the Thirty-nine Articles expresses this point more specifically:

---

8  The Eleven Articles, Article 3, in Bray, *Documents of the English Reformation*, p. 349.
9  Article 3, pp. 349-50.

The Church hath power to decree Rites or Ceremonies and authority in Controversies of Faith: And yet it is not lawful for the Church to ordain any thing that is contrary to God's Word written, neither may it so expound one place of Scripture, that it be repugnant to another. Wherefore, although the Church be a witness and a keeper of holy Writ, yet, as it ought not to decree anything against the same, so besides the same ought it not to enforce anything to be believed for necessity of Salvation.

Also in the Thirty-nine Articles is found a statement in Article 6 that the Bishop of Rome has no more authority than other bishops have in their provinces and dioceses, and that his claim to be supreme head of the universal Church of Christ is 'a usurped power, contrary to the Scriptures and the Word of God, and contrary to the example of the primitive Church'.

Despite this robust language, the question of whether the church in England had had the right to make this decision exercised the minds of many in the sixteenth century. A guiding principle in their response was a sense of being called by God to re-establish the apostolic – and thus true – Church. In his *Apology for the Church of England* (1562), John Jewel conceded that although the Church of England had 'departed from that Church which these men call Catholic, ... we are come, as near as we possibly could, to the church of the apostles and of the old Catholic bishops and fathers'.[10] Since no council could speak for the whole world, the church in England had 'sought to remedy our own Church by a provincial synod'.[11] Jewel acknowledged that some said that this should not have been done without the Bishop of Rome's commandment, but, he pointed out, 'so the

---

10  John Jewel, *An Apology of the Church of England* in J. Ayre (ed.), *The Works of John Jewel* (Cambridge: Cambridge University Press/Parker Society, 1848), Vol. 1, p. 100.

11  Jewel, *Apology*, p. 101.

case stood, unless we left him, we could not come to Christ'.[12] Only by leaving what was deemed by Rome the 'Catholic' Church, had the Church in England been able to rejoin the true Catholic Church. This did not imply a complete rejection of the Roman Church: as Hooker would put it towards the end of the sixteenth century:

> even as the Apostle doth say of Israel that they are in one respect enemies but in another beloved of God, in like sort with Rome we dare not communicate concerning sundry her gross and grievous abominations, yet touching those main points of Christian truth wherein they constantly still persist, we gladly acknowledge them to be of the family of Jesus Christ.[13]

Throughout the sixteenth century, there is evidence of a struggle to recognize where the true Church is, and to take account of the different ways in which that true Church might manifest itself.

The Canons of the Church of England drawn up in 1603/4 stand firmly in this tradition. The Canons affirm the Church of England as 'a true and apostolical Church', and the King's supremacy over that Church; they censor those who impugn 'the King's Supremacy', 'the publick worship of God established in the Church of England', 'the Articles of Religion', 'the Rites and Ceremonies', 'its form of government by Archbishops, Bishops etc.', 'the Ordinal' and other characteristic aspects of the Church of England, along with 'organisers of conventicles' and 'those who cause schism'.[14] The Canons manifest the Church's

---

12  Jewel, *Apology of the Church of England*, p. 103.
13  Richard Hooker, *Of the Laws of Ecclesiastical Polity* in John Keble (ed.), *The Works of Richard Hooker* (Oxford: Clarendon Press: 1841), Vol. 1, p. 283.
14  See the headings of titles of Canons 1 and 2, Canons of 1603 (1604), in Gerald Bray (ed.), *The Anglican Canons 1529–1947*, Church of

conviction that it may legislate and order its own life. The earlier English version of the Canons is often slightly different from the Latin version; where the Latin departs from the English, it replaces a condemnation with a positive statement. Thus, the heading of the English text of Canon 8 focuses on those who dissent from the practice of the Church of England – 'Impugners of the form of consecrating and ordering archbishops, bishops, etc. in the Church of England, censured' – whilst the Latin form declares the ordinal to be 'consonant with the word of God'.[15] This first section of the 1603 (Latin)/1604 (English) Canons is intended to buttress the Church of England's understanding of itself as the catholic Church in England, and to affirm its liturgy and its ministry. The affirmation of the orthodoxy of the ordinal is at the same time an affirmation that those ordained bishop, priest or deacon by the Church of England are indeed bishops, priests and deacons, and that nobody, on pain of excommunication, is to account them otherwise.

The Church of England could legitimately define the structure of its ministry and its ordination service precisely because it was the true manifestation of the Church catholic in England. English divines generally conceived the relation of the wider catholic Church to the particular Churches, in terms of geography. Thus John Sharp, Archbishop of York, writing in 1688 of the catholic Church:

> whenever we name or speak of the Catholic Church, (if we will take the Scripture notion) we must mean by that word, the whole multitude of christians throughout the world that are imbodied [*sic*] into one society by baptism and the profession of the Christian faith, and the

---

England Record Society 6 (Woodbridge: The Boydell Press, 1998), pp. 262–81.

15  Bray, *Anglican Canons*, pp. 275–8. Canon 8 of the 1603/4 Canons is the predecessor of the Canon A4 of the current canons of the Church of England.

participation of the common means of salvation. But when we speak of a church of any single denomination, as the Greek Church, the Ethiopic Church, the Roman Church, the English Church, or the like, we mean only some particular church which is but a part of the church catholic or universal.[16]

For Sharp, the term 'Church' as used in scripture, always means:

the whole company of Christians dispersed all over the world, who profess the common faith (though perhaps none of them without mixture of error) and enjoy the administration of the word and sacrament under their lawful pastors and governors.[17]

Within that particularity, wrote William Wake, Archbishop of Canterbury, in 1718:

The Ch. of England as a national Ch. has all that power within Herselfe, over her own members, which is necessary to enable her to settle her doctrine, Government and Discipline, according to the will of Xt, and the edification of her members. We have no concern for other Xn. Chs. more yn that of charity, and to keep up the unity of the Catholic Ch. in the Communion of Sts.[18]

---

16  John Sharp, 'A discussion of the question which the Roman Catholics much insist upon with the protestants, viz. In which of the different communions in Christendom, the only Church of Christ is found' (1686), in: *The Works of the Most Revd Dr John Sharp* (London: Knapton, Longman, 1754), Vol. 7, p. 96.

17  Sharp, 'the different communions in Christendom,' p. 97.

18  L. Adams (ed.), *William Wake's Gallican Correspondence and related Documents* (New York: Peter Lang, 1988–91), Vol. 1, p. 100. Abbreviations in original.

The French Church, he writes, could do this too, 'if it would in good earnest throw off the Pope's pretensions'.[19] And because of this, those who crossed national boundaries should be treated as members of the one Church. Of the licensing of a Scottish Presbyterian to minister in England, he wrote: 'I should be unwilling to affirm that where the ministry is not episcopal there is no church, nor any true administration of the sacraments.'[20]

For most of its history, the Church of England has expressed its ecclesiology in national terms. This was articulated in the establishing of the Jerusalem Bishopric in 1841:

> It is the will of the Lord, that there should be distinct families of nations while His Church is militant upon earth. He has, therefore, willed that there should be national churches, invested as individuals are with mutual accountability.[21]

The catholicity of the Church offered a balance to the national aspects of its actual manifestations: 'Catholicity renders the union of several Churches practicable; nationality prevents vital unity in the Church from degenerating into the similitude of death.'[22] The later nineteenth century saw increasing interest in the ways in which the particularity of national churches could discover themselves to be manifestations of the Church catholic.[23]

The competence of the Church of England to act in matters pertaining to the ordering of its ministry has been a principle since

---

19 Adams, *Wake's Gallican Correspondence*, Vol. 1, p. 100.
20 Adams, *Wake's Gallican Correspondence*, Vol. 5, p. 57.
21 William H. Hechler (ed.), *The Jerusalem Bishopric Documents* (London: Trübner, 1883), p. 32.
22 Hechler, *Jerusalem Bishopric Documents*, pp. 28, 30.
23 For reflections on aspects of catholicity thus discovered, see: Charlotte Methuen, '"From all nations and languages": Reflections on Church, Catholicity and Culture', in Mark D. Chapman (ed.), *The Anglican Covenant: Unity and Diversity in the Anglican Communion* (London: Mowbray, 2008), pp. 123–42.

its establishment in the sixteenth century. According to that principle, it has been clear to members of the Church of England that their church was not only competent to pronounce on questions of doctrine and order, but that it must indeed do so, for the Church of England is the true expression of Christ's Church in this place. The principle of mutual accountability cannot be taken lightly in making such pronouncements. But neither should the possibility of a call to prophetic action be dismissed: for one particular manifestation of the Church catholic may indeed be called to proclaim a fresh understanding of the gospel, and so to preach the word of God to the wider Church.

# 4

## Women Bishops?
## Views in the Roman Catholic Church, Official and
## Otherwise

JOHN WIJNGAARDS

The Roman Catholic Church is a vast body of more than a billion believers. It is an organization creaking in its joints, straddled as it lies on all continents, battered by secularization and local pressures, torn by internal conflict on much-needed reforms. Held together by vigorous control from its Vatican centre it gives the appearance of almost monolithic unity. Nothing is further from the truth.

However, the future of the Catholic Church does not lie in its organization, but in its soul, in the faith and faith images of its believers. And that future is bright for women in holy orders, for reasons I will briefly outline.

### 1 Reasons of the Mind

The theological thinking on episcopacy and women in the Roman Catholic Church can be grouped under three headings:

a. pronouncements by Church Councils
b. the official doctrinal teaching emanating from the Vatican
c. the opinions of the academic community of theologians

#### a Pronouncements by Church Councils

Since the Reformation, and initially in response to it, Church Councils have stressed the unity of the sacrament of holy orders. The Council of Trent declared during its 23rd Session on the sacrament of ordination, on 15 July 1563:

> Canon 6: If anyone says that in the Catholic Church
> there is not a hierarchy by divine ordination instituted,
> consisting of bishops, priests, and deacons; let him be
> anathema.
>
> Canon 7: If anyone says, that bishops are not superior to
> priests; or, that they have not the power of confirming
> and ordaining; or, that the power which they possess is
> common to them and to priests, etc. etc. let him be
> anathema.[1]

This was interpreted as meaning that bishops rank higher than
priests, but share in the same sacrament.

The Second Vatican Council, while correcting many one-sided
medieval and scholastic views on the episcopacy and the
priesthood, basically reaffirmed their fundamental oneness. For
example, in its decree *Christus Dominus* of 28 October 1965 it
states:

> Bishops enjoy the fullness of the sacrament of orders and
> both priests and deacons are dependent upon them in the
> exercise of their authority. For the priests are the prudent
> fellow workers of the episcopal order and are themselves
> consecrated as true priests of the New Testament, just as
> deacons are ordained for the ministry and serve the
> people of God in communion with the bishop and his
> presbytery.[2]

According to the most authoritative Catholic sources, therefore,
priesthood and episcopacy are so closely united in the unity of
holy orders and the unity of the local church round their bishop,

---

1   Heinrich Denzinger, *Enchiridion Symbolorum* (Freiburg: Herder,
    1955), nos 963, 964.
2   *Christus Dominus*, §15, in Austin Flannery, *Vatican Council II* (New
    York: Costello, 1988), p. 571.

that the question of women bishops and women priests are one and the same question.

## b. *Vatican official doctrinal teaching*

This approach is clearly demonstrated in doctrinal documents emanating from the Congregation for the Doctrine of the Faith in Rome, and at times from the pope himself. In the decrees that exclude women from the priesthood, the episcopacy is either not mentioned at all, or mentioned in one breath with the priesthood. I will highlight examples from the main documents.[3]

The document with the most detailed argumentation, *Inter Insigniores* (15 October 1976), and the accompanying commentary, only mention the episcopacy once, namely in this passage: 'the bishop or the priest, in the exercise of his ministry, does not act in his own name, *in persona propria:* he represents Christ' (§ 25). The quotation is said to derive from Saint Cyprian, who – interestingly – only mentions the priest. *Mulieris Dignitatem* (30 September 1988), which emphatically excludes women from the priesthood, does not mention the episcopate. Neither does *Ordinatio Sacerdotalis* (22 May 1994) that declared the exclusion to be 'definitive teaching'.

The *Catechism of the Catholic Church* (1994) mentions them in one breath:

> Only a baptized man (*vir*) validly received sacred ordination. The Lord Jesus chose men (*viri*) to form the college of the twelve apostles, and the apostles did the same when they chose collaborators to succeed them in their ministry. The college of bishops, with whom the priests are united in the priesthood, makes the college of the twelve an ever-present and ever-active reality until Christ's return. The Church recognizes herself to be

---

3    The full texts are available on my website: www.womenpriests.org

bound by this choice made by the Lord himself. For this
reason the ordination of women is not possible.[4]

The ordination of women to the priesthood and to the episcopacy
are, therefore, one and the same question for the official Church.
If women can be priests, they can be bishops since the two are
inseparable.

This position, in fact, creates a major problem for the Magisterium. The unity of the sacrament of ordination also covers the
diaconate. Given that a number of international scholars have
amply documented the sacramental ordination of women as
deacons during the first nine centuries,[5] this means that women
can, in principle, also be ordained priests and bishops. This is the
reason why the Vatican refuses to reinstate the ancient diaconate.

*c. The opinions of the academic community of theologians*

In the community of Roman Catholic theologians I have not seen
much, if any, evidence of trying to separate the episcopacy and
the priesthood in the context of the question of women's
ordination. This is in contrast to the question of the diaconate. On
that topic, some theologians contend that it would be perfectly
possible for the Roman Catholic Church to separate the two
ministries in such a way that women could be given the sacrament
of the diaconate, even though the priesthood was withheld from
them. This is, for instance, the opinion of the Orthodox Bishop
Kallistos Ware[6] and the Catholic theologians Peter Hünermann,[7]

4   *Catechism of the Catholic Church* (London: Geoffrey Chapman, 1994),
    pp. 353–4.
5   John Wijngaards, *No Women in Holy Orders? The Women Deacons of
    the Early Church* (Norwich: Canterbury Press, 2002): see extensive
    bibliographies on pp. 137–43; 211–14.
6   Kallistos Ware, 'Man, Woman and the Priesthood of Christ', in
    Thomas Hopko (ed.), *Women and the Priesthood* (Crestwood, NY: St
    Vladimir's Seminary Press, 1983), pp. 9–37.

Dorothea Reininger[8], and Phyllis Zagano.[9] I believe that they are
mistaken for two important reasons: a historical one and a
Church-political one. However, the admission to the episcopate
and the priesthood will not so easily be separated in the Roman
Catholic Church. For the community of Catholic theologians the
simple issue is this: are the arguments for excluding women from
ordination given by the Vatican valid or not? Did Jesus Christ
establish a norm by only choosing men in the initial twelve
apostles? Did the subsequent reluctance to ordain women in the
Church derive from cultural prejudices, or from an awareness of a
presumed divine and revealed injunction originating in Jesus
himself? The answer determines the fate of women deacons,
priests and bishops – all in one stroke.

By all evidence available to me, I estimate that three-quarters of
Catholic theologians disagree with the official position held by the
Vatican. They do not accept as proven that Jesus Christ himself
excluded women from future ministries. They point to the cultural
bias against women as the reason for the anti-female decisions
taken throughout the tradition. I have said, 'by all evidence
available to me', since a blanket of silence has descended on the
theological community after *Ordinatio Sacerdotalis*, which
effectively forbade discussion on the question. Moreover, the
Vatican is trying to fill all important positions with candidates
who favour its own views. Bishops are chosen only if they have

---

7    Peter Hünermann, 'Conclusions Regarding the Female Diaconate',
     in *Theological Studies* 36 (1975), pp. 325–33, here pp. 327–8;
     'Diakonat – ein Beitrag zur Erneuerung des kirchlichen Amtes?
     Wider-Holung', in *Diakonia Christi* 29 (1994), pp. 13–22; 'Lehramt-
     liche Dokumente zur Frauenordination', in Walter Gross (ed.),
     *Frauenordination* (Munich: Wewel, 1996), pp. 83–96; 'Theologische
     Argumente für die Diakonatsweihe von Frauen', in *Diakonat. Ein
     Amt für Frauen in der Kirche – Ein frauengerechtes Amt?* (Ostfildern:
     Schwabenverlag, 1997), pp. 98–128.
8    Dorothea Reininger, *Diakonat der Frau in der Einen Kirche* (Ostfildern:
     Schwabenverlag, 1999).
9    Phyllis Zagano, *Holy Saturday* (New York: Crossroad, 2000).

first indicated that they agree with the Vatican. Parish priests and theologians in church institutions have to swear an oath of loyalty that implies agreement with the Vatican. The Congregation for the Doctrine of the Faith follows up these measures by censuring anyone who steps out of line. The Vatican criticizes bishops in person if they have organizations in their jurisdiction that favour women priests. The Vatican sends letters to bishops ordering them to discipline church personnel who support women's ordination. All this happens despite the solemn promise by the Second Vatican Council that 'all the faithful, both clerical and lay, should be accorded a lawful freedom of inquiry, freedom of thought and freedom of expression'.[10]

As a result of Vatican pressure, many Roman Catholic theologians do not publicly discuss the issue. But it is possible to gauge what they think from personal correspondence and contacts through such organizations as the Catholic Theological Association of Great Britain, the Catholic Theological Association of Europe and the Catholic Theological Society of America. The credibility of the Magisterium's banning women from ordination borders on zero: scholars agree with Hans Küng, not with Joseph Ratzinger. It can thus be shown that the arguments of the central teaching authority regarding women and holy orders are rejected by the majority of Catholic theologians. The situation is not unlike that in the Soviet Union before the collapse of communism, when no self-respecting economist agreed with the doctrinal position of the establishment.

## 2 Reasons of the Heart

Theological debate on women's admission to holy orders, however suppressed, is not the only reality of the moment; perhaps not even the most crucial one. Underneath rational arguments for or against, another conflict is present that will, in my view, prove far more dangerous to the Vatican's intransigence regarding women. The conflict I am referring to is that between

---

10  *Gaudium et Spes*, §62 in Flannery, *Vatican Council II*, p. 968.

the Vatican claim that Jesus Christ can only be represented by a male, and the deepseated, truly 'Catholic', conviction that God most intimately relates to us through female images.

*Religion and preconscious symbols*

The study of religion in a number of disciplines has shown that religion is not defined so much by doctrines as by images. It is a preconscious activity beginning in that edge of our personality where our consciousness fades off into unconsciousness. Religion has its origins in that borderland of consciousness where metaphors and stories, images and symbols, daydreams and fantasies occur. As Clifford Geertz puts it in his classic definition: 'Religion is a system of symbols.'[11] Further studies have narrowed this down by showing that people have two principal kinds of religious experience. The first is a merging in God as the source of our being; the second is an encounter with God as the totally other.

*The contemplative experience* exemplifies the first approach. God is perceived as a mystery underlying the whole of reality as we know it. God is the 'immanent ground and operative principle of all being'.[12] We try to unite ourselves to God by partaking in sacred images, by climbing God's mountain or bathing in God's sacred river; or simply by honouring the symbol that mediates God's presence. In its highest forms this approach leads to mysticism. It is based on our experience of our mother.[13]

*The prophetic approach*, on the other hand, experiences God as a person, usually male, who has revealed a message and who imposes his commands. By word and divine will God compels us

---

11  Clifford Geertz, *The Interpretation of Cultures* (New York: Basic Books, 1973).

12  S. Radakrishnan, *The Hindu View of Life* (London: Macmillan, 1927), pp. 24–5.

13  E. H. Erikson, *Identity* (New York: Norton, 1968), pp. 96ff.; Heije Faber, *Cirkelen om een geheim* (Boom: Meppel, 1972); Wil Veldhuis, *Geloof en Ervaring* (Bilthoven: Ambo, 1973), pp. 11–16.

either to accept or reject his lordship. His revelation comes through human mediators and addresses itself to concrete human realities. God is experienced as the unexpected, the totally other, the one to whom the believer submits in an act of obedience and surrender.[14]

Both forms of religious experience have their roots in crucial stages of our psychological growth. That is why they come so naturally to us and why we feel the need of both the one and the other. But there is no doubt that either the mother-experience or the father-experience of God predominates in individuals and in religious systems.[15]

*The characteristically 'Catholic' imagination*

Some of the marked differences between the Catholic and the Protestant experience of Christian faith can be seen in the religious context I have so briefly sketched above. David Tracy's seminal study, *The Analogical Imagination*, posits that the Catholic imagination is 'analogical', i.e. based on image, and the Protestant imagination is 'dialectical', that is: based on word. The Catholic Christian experience assumes a God who is present in the world, a self-disclosing God in and through creation. The world and all its events, objects and people tend to be somewhat like God. The Protestant Christian experience, on the other hand, assumes a God who is radically different from the world and who discloses him/her self only on rare occasions (especially in Jesus

---

14 K. A. H. Hidding, *De Evolutie van het godsdienstig bewustzijn* (Utrecht: het Spectrum, 1965); Heije Faber, 'Wisselende patronen van religieuze ervaring', in *Tijdschrift voor Theologie* 11 (1971), pp. 225–48.

15 Alister Hardy, *The Divine Flame* (London: Collins, 1966), pp. 156–75; *The Spiritual Nature of Man* (Oxford: Clarendon Press, 1979), pp. 134–6. Hardy traces the two approaches even further back in evolution, relating them to two social bonds rooted in natural animal dependence on the mother and submissive attachment to the dominant leader of the pack.

Christ and him crucified). The world and all its events, objects and people tend to be radically dissimilar from God.

The Catholic tends to see society as a 'sacrament' of God, a set of ordered relationships, governed by both justice and love, that reveal, however imperfectly, the presence of God. Society is 'natural' and 'good', and people's 'natural' response to God is social. The Protestant, on the other hand, tends to see human society as 'God-forsaken' and therefore unnatural and oppressive. The individual stands over against society and is not integrated into it.[16]

These approximations, always in danger of being overplayed, nevertheless explain a verifiable fact. Protestants treasure the inspired word. Their churches are austere, with the pulpit at their centre; they pursue Christian holiness in a hostile world. Catholics love images and pictures, colourful churches with statues of saints, devotions that speak to the heart, ritual rather than sermons. The American sociologist Andrew Greeley has shown in further studies that this 'Catholic imagination' has far-reaching consequences for the way God is perceived.[17] In other words: in the Catholic imagination the mother experience predominates. God is touched through sacraments, images and symbols. God is seen more easily in feminine images, of which Our Lady, the 'Mother of God', is a reflected example.

*The clash between image and authority*

Having taking you on such a lengthy detour, I can now come to the specific point I want to make. Image stands at the centre of the Catholic tradition. Image featured prominently in the clashes regarding icons during the eighth and ninth centuries and at the Reformation. Catholic tradition has always affirmed that God has overturned the Old Testament ban against images by revealing

---

16 David Tracy, *The Analogical Imagination. Christian Theology and the Culture of Pluralism* (London: SCM Press, 1981).

17 Andrew Greeley, *The Catholic Myth. The Behavior and Beliefs of American Catholics* (New York: Scribner's, 1990), pp. 41–52.

himself in Jesus Christ, in sacraments and in ritual. Regarding women, image again stands at the centre.

The Roman Catholic Church is at the moment in the grip of a rigid, masculine, patriarchal system of control. This heavy-handed masculine hierarchy has, moreover, proclaimed a monopoly over the image of God: 'Only a male can represent Christ at the eucharist.' In *Mulieris Dignitatem*, Pope John Paul II even uttered the assertion, never before made in the Church, that Jesus Christ had *to become incarnate as a male* – to represent the Father – and that therefore only a man can be his (and the Father's) image at the eucharist:

> The bridegroom – the Son consubstantial with the Father as God – became the son of Mary; he became the "son of man", true man, a male. The symbol of the bridegroom is masculine. ... It is the Eucharist above all that expresses the redemptive act of Christ, the bridegroom, toward the church, the bride. This is clear and unambiguous when the sacramental ministry of the Eucharist, in which the priest acts *in persona Christi*, is performed by a man. This explanation confirms the teaching of the declaration *Inter Insigniores*, published at the behest of Paul VI in response to the question concerning the admission of women to the ministerial priesthood.[18]

This claim clashes directly with the deep seated experience of Catholics that they touch God in feminine images. Indeed, the absence of women at the altar went largely unnoticed in the past, when patriarchalism was the dominant cultural climate. Things have now changed. Our present-day renewed social awareness is waking up more and more women and men to the intolerable absence of women as representatives of Christ presiding at the eucharist. The clash manifests itself in many Catholics saying spontaneously: 'I'm sure that this is not what Jesus wanted, nor is

---

18  *Mulieris Dignitatem* (15 August 1988).

it what God wants now.' The mismatch angers women. It makes many men uneasy, including bishops and priests. This sense of anger and unease, which is difficult to define precisely, has considerable ecclesial significance.

The Second Vatican Council has stressed that the carrier of inerrancy is the *sensus fidei* that rests within the body of the Church:

> The entire body of the faithful, anointed as they are by the Holy One, cannot err in matters of belief. They manifest this special property by means of the whole people's supernatural discernment in matters of faith when 'from the Bishops down to the last of the lay faithful' they show universal agreement in matters of faith and morals.[19]

An amendment proposed at Vatican II to the effect that the infallibility of the Magisterium is the source of the people's infallibility was rejected by the Council as being contrary to tradition. The Pope and the College of Bishops have the role of articulating matters of faith and morals through their authoritative teaching. However, this exercise is grounded in the infallibility of the whole people of God, not the other way about.[20]

As John Henry Newman pointed out when describing latent tradition, a truth or value carried by the *sensus fidei* does not need to be clearly articulated in order to be valid.

> The absence, or partial absence, or incompleteness of dogmatic statements is no proof of the absence of impressions or implicit judgements, in the mind of the

---

19 *Lumen Gentium*, Dogmatic Constitution on the Church, 21 November 1964, §12.

20 Vatican II, *Acta Synodalia* III/I, pp. 198–9; R. R. Gaillardetz, *Teaching with Authority: A Theology of the Magisterium in the Church* (Collegeville: Liturgical Press, 1997), p. 154.

Church. Even centuries might pass without the formal expression of a truth, which had been all along the secret life of millions of faithful souls.[21]

Recent studies have reiterated the ancient tradition, reaffirmed in Vatican II, that a doctrine proposed by the teaching authority needs to be received by the body of the faithful to be fully authenticated. The faithful, therefore, have a role not only in providing initial impulses on formulating a new understanding of doctrine but also through a process of feedback.[22]

This means that the Vatican attempt to make the living image of Christ in priests and bishops a male preserve is ultimately doomed to fail. Catholic consciousness will not tolerate it. Doctrinal pronouncements will be overturned by faith in the heart.

---

21  John Henry Newman, 'A University Sermon Preached on the Purification', in *Sermons* (Oxford: Parker, 1843); see also his 'On Consulting the Faithful in Matters of Doctrine', published originally in *The Rambler* (July 1859).

22  Richard R. Gaillardetz, 'The Reception of Doctrine: New Perspectives', in Bernard Hoose (ed.), *Authority in the Roman Catholic Church* (Aldershot: Ashgate, 2002), pp. 95–114; see also http://www.womenpriests.org/teaching/gaill6.asp

# 5

## Methodism and Women Bishops

DAVID CARTER

### Methodism and Women Bishops

In recent years Methodism has given an unequivocal answer to the question of the ordination of women to the episcopate based upon its view that all offices in the Church, both lay and ordained, should be open to both sexes. Thus, we support the ordination of women to the episcopate within the Church of England. We are naturally quite clear also that if there are to be bishops within the British Methodist Church, then such an episcopate must be open to both men and women.[1]

Our major sister Methodist church, the United Methodist Church of USA is an episcopally ordered church, its ministry, like those of the church of Denmark and the Porvoo Agreement

---

1    In 2005 a joint working party of the Faith and Order Committee and the Methodist Council (the latter being the equivalent within Methodism of the Archbishops' Council for the Church of England) submitted a report to the Conference entitled *What Sort of Bishops? Models of Episcopacy and British Methodism* (posted at: http://www.methodist.org.uk/static/conf2005/co_60_whatsortofbi shops_0805.doc), containing a series of reflections on *episcope* and episcopacy plus varying recommendations as to what sort of ministers might become bishops: e.g. presidents of Conference, district chairs, some superintendents, etc. §48 asserts again the principle that all ministries, including any future episcopate within British Methodism, should be open to both sexes. The Conference of 2005 commended these proposals for study and will make a decision on whether to act on them (and, if so, on which particular alternative) in 2007.

churches of Norway and Iceland, deriving ultimately from ordination by a presbyter: in the Methodist case, John Wesley. The United Methodist Church (UMC) started to ordain women as 'elders' (the term used for presbyter in our sister church) a little earlier than British Methodism. In 2002, there were eight women bishops amongst the 50 bishops of the UMC.

The principle of the equality of the sexes in church office was clearly stated in the international Roman Catholic–Methodist dialogue. That dialogue has throughout been characterized by the holding in tension of three things: (1) commitment to ultimate unity in faith, life and mission; (2) a desire to receive spiritual riches and insights from each other; and (3) a frankness concerning continuing difficulties which currently seem insoluble.[2] Thus in the report *The Apostolic Tradition*, we read:

> Methodists ordain women because they believe that women also receive the call, evidenced by inward conviction and outward manifestation of the gifts and graces and confirmed by the gathering of the faithful.

---

2   For an excellent account of the dialogue, which began at the same time as ARCIC, see David Chapman, *In Search of the Catholic Spirit, Methodists and Roman Catholics in Dialogue* (Peterborough: Epworth Press, 2004). The dialogue at both the national and international level has throughout been characterized by great mutual respect and friendship, but also by the clear, if reluctant, acceptance that there are matters on which the two churches cannot currently agree. Nevertheless, they have much in common: in particular, the emphasis upon the necessary interdependence within the universal Church of all local churches, the doctrine of holiness, and the emphasis upon holistic mission. The dialogue deserves to be much better known both within the Roman Catholic and Methodist churches and amongst our partners. The most recent report, with a strong emphasis upon the exchange of gifts, is *The Grace Given you in Christ: Catholics and Methodists Reflect Further on the Church* (Lake Junaluska: World Methodist Council, 2006).

Catholics do not ordain women, believing that they have
no authority to change a practice that belongs to the
sacrament of order as received in the Tradition of the
Church.[3]

It will be noted that the Methodist statement gives particular
emphasis to the historic and present-day experience of the
Methodist people. Whilst Methodists would never privilege
experience over scripture, and would be wary of citing their
experience were it to clash with that of most of the rest of
Christendom, there is no doubt that the fact that women have
been able to exercise a provenly effective ministry of oversight at a
level where they have the care of other ministers and several or
many congregations weighs heavily with Methodists. This is true
both within the British and other Methodist churches and within
other churches, including, of course, some provinces of the
Anglican Communion and some of the Porvoo Lutheran
churches.

British Methodism reinforced the teaching noted above at the
time of its 1998 Conference when, in the course of giving its
approval to the continuation of the conversations that ultimately
led to the present Anglican–Methodist Covenant, it asserted that
Methodism believed that every church office should be open to
persons of both sexes.

**Methodism and Women's Ordination**

A number of points, however, should be made clear: while
Methodism has long accepted the case for the ordination of
women, it has also been sensitive to the ecumenical dimension of
the question, in respect of the presbyterate as well as the

---

3    The Apostolic Tradition, report of fifth quinquennium of the
     International Roman Catholic Methodist Commission, §§96, 97,
     cited in Jeffrey Gros, Harding Meyer, William Rusch, *Growth in
     Agreement II: Reports and Agreed Statements of Ecumenical Conversations
     on a World Level, 1982–1998* (Geneva: WCC, 2000), Vol. II, p. 616.

episcope. As early as the 1930s, the Methodist Conference could see no *theological* objection to the ordination of women to the ministry of word and sacrament.[4] In the very different circumstances of those days, when Methodist ministers were still subject to a practically as well as theoretically rigid discipline of itinerancy, it was suggested that it would be impossible for married women to be itinerant and that therefore marriage would have to result in their resignation from active work. In other words, *active* female (but not male!) ministers would have to be celibate.

In the immediate aftermath of the war, the question of ordaining women was little discussed. When it resurfaced in the 1960s, British methodism was preoccupied with the Anglican–Methodist Conversations that had arisen out of Archbishop Fisher's famous initiative in 1946 when he invited the free churches to consider 'taking episcopacy into their system'. It was then tacitly agreed that the question of women's ordained ministry should be left for joint resolution between the two churches after the consummation of Stage 1 of the envisaged unity scheme. It was only when this did not materialize, after finally failing to get the necessary vote in General Synod in 1972, that British Methodism went ahead and admitted women candidates to the presbyterate in 1974.

A second example of ecumenical sensitivity was shown more recently at the time of the abortive scheme for an ecumenical bishop in east Cardiff. It was agreed, with some reluctance, to meet the sensitivities of many in the Church in Wales by accepting that the first person nominated to such an office should be male, provided the post was thereafter open to both men and women. Sadly, this did not win enough support for the scheme in the Church in Wales.

Methodists are thus not unaware of the ecumenical sensitivities involved. For some of us, those sensitivities are still particularly

---

4   *Statements and Reports of the Methodist Church on Faith and Order* (Peterborough: Epworth Press, 1984), Vol. 1, pp. 117–23.

acute. Under the terms of the Anglican–Methodist Covenant, we are committed to 'listen to each other and to take account of each others' concerns, especially in areas that affect our relationship as churches'.[5] I have frequently argued to my fellow Methodists that this involves a sympathetic and empathic concern for the whole range of views within the Church of England, including a kind and pastoral concern for those Anglicans with whom we feel bound to disagree, whether on issues of women's ministry or otherwise. We have the delicate and difficult task of praying and working for the ever deeper unity of our two complex and pluralist churches. Unity in reconciled diversity is increasingly required *within* particular churches as well as *between* them.

It may help to give some background, first to the question of women's ministry overall within Methodism and then to say a little about Methodist attitudes to the possible reception of the sign of the episcopal succession.

A few Methodist women were involved in preaching even in the time of the Wesleys. John Wesley did not approve and aimed to limit their ministry purely to the service of their fellow women; he was happy for them to 'exhort' other women and to act as class leaders for exclusively female classes. In 1803 the Wesleyan Methodist Conference, very sensitive to any action that might appear revolutionary or subversive in that era, banned preaching by women even as local (i.e. lay) preachers. However, many women did continue to act as class leaders, some of them women of great spiritual qualities, sometimes referred to in obituaries in the *Wesleyan Magazine* as 'mothers in Israel'.

Women, however, played a more significant role in two newer Methodist movements which developed in the early nineteenth century: Primitive Methodism and the Bible Christian Connexion. Both these movements, in their earlier phases, were less

---

5   *An Anglican–Methodist Covenant: Common Statement of the Formal Conversations between the Methodist Church of Great Britain and the Church of England* (London: Methodist Publishing House and Church House Publishing, 2001), p. 61.

tied to social conservatism than was the original Wesleyan Connexion, and were more concerned with whether a preacher had the 'gifts and graces' for the work, to use the traditional Methodist phrase. The Bible Christians from around 1815 to 1820 had almost equal numbers of male and female itinerant preachers. They justified their practice in terms of the famous prophecy of Joel, cited in Acts in its description of the coming of the Spirit on the day of Pentecost: 'and your sons and your daughters shall prophesy' (Acts 2.17).

In an article written some years ago, the veteran Roman Catholic ecumenist George Tavard referred to the first ordination of a woman to the ministry of word and sacrament as having taken place in New England in 1853.[6] The first *recognition* of women in such a role took place almost 40 years earlier amongst the Bible Christians and the Primitive Methodists. Ordination by prayer and the laying-on of hands was not at that stage part of the practice of those two churches.[7] Many of the women only

---

6   'The Ordination of Women', in *One in Christ* 3 (1987), pp. 200–11.

7   In this context, it is worth remembering that even the Wesleyan Methodists did not ordain by the laying-on of hands until 1836, in their case out of a desire to avoid strengthening the breach with the Church of England which so many of them deeply regretted. In all the Methodist connexions, the act of ministerial commissioning included the solemn reception into full connexion by the standing vote of the Conference. This is still Methodist practice today. The Conference resolves to receive into full connexion those that have been trained and satisfactorily completed their 'probation'. It also resolves that they be ordained by prayer and the laying-on of hands, the ordination usually following in the evening after the solemn vote of reception into full connexion. Ordination in British Methodism is carried out by a president or ex-president of the Conference with the help of assisting ministers. In American Methodism ordination is exercised by a bishop, but in both cases under the corporate authority of the Conference which exercises final corporate *episcope*. Conference would continue to authorize ordination in the event of British Methodism receiving the sign of the episcopal succession. Though bishops would be the principal ministers in ordination, they

'travelled' a few years. The last of the Primitive Methodist women preachers, Elizabeth Bultitude, however, travelled until 1862 before receiving a retirement annuity. She continued to be regarded as a minister until her death in 1890.

Victorian respectability and the contemporary emphasis upon the separate spheres of men and women meant that the Wesleyan Connexion eschewed the example of the more radical groups, and no woman was ordained in any of the branches of British Methodism between 1890 and 1974. However, some overseas Methodist Conferences were quicker off the mark after the Second World War in ordaining women. I know of at least one British Methodist woman who went to the United States because she was convinced of a call to the ordained ministry that could not then be fulfilled in Britain.

When women were finally admitted to the British Methodist ministry in 1974, the old reservations about how to handle the problem of marriage had largely disappeared, the social context having changed radically since the 1930s. Those married women presbyters whose responsibilities towards young families make it impossible for them to be in pastoral charge are now able to be temporarily 'without appointment' (as was the case with the wife of the previous superintendent minister of my own circuit).

A substantial number from the first cohorts of female candidates for the presbyterate came from the ranks of the former Wesley Deaconess Order, many of whose members had long been aware of a call to presbyteral ministry that they could not earlier fulfil. Others stayed in the Order which was, a few years later, temporarily closed and subsequently reopened to candidates of both sexes as the diaconal order. The Methodist Deed of Union, which had previously recognized only one order of ministry amongst Methodists, was altered in 1993 and Methodism now has two orders of ordained ministry, the presbyteral and the

---

would only be authorized to ordain those previously approved by the Conference.

diaconal.[8] There are currently still some differences between the theology and practice of the diaconate as understood in Methodism and in the Church of England. These are outlined in the book *An Anglican–Methodist Covenant* and are the subject of ongoing discussion within the Joint Implementation Committee responsible for overseeing the working of the Covenant and for looking at ways of closer advance towards fuller unity.[9] The Anglican–Methodist Covenant acknowledges that 'we affirm that there already exists a basis for agreement on the principles of episcopal oversight as a visible sign and instrument of the communion of the Church in time and space'.[10]

## Methodism and Episcopacy

It is important to realize that Methodism, unlike some other Protestant traditions, has never denied the legitimacy *per se* of

---

8  A tangled situation with regard to the diaconate existed before this change with the ordination service for the diaconate implying one thing and the Deed of Union another. Interestingly, the first statements on the possibility of the ordination of women to the ministry of word and sacrament had talked of Methodism already having an order of ministry for women in the then Wesley Deaconess Order.

9  *An Anglican–Methodist Covenant*, pp. 45–6. A major point is that Anglicans always ordain to the diaconate before ordination to the presbyterate, whereas Methodists ordain candidates for presbyteral ministry directly to that order without previous diaconal ordination which is conferred only on candidates for the diaconate. When I recently discussed this problem with a Roman Catholic expert, Fr Paul McPartlan, he told me that practice seems to have varied in the pre-Nicene Church and that the current practices of British and American Methodism could both claim some precedent from that era. Until recently, the Amercian United Methodist Church kept to Anglican practice with future elders first being ordained deacon, but I gather this practice is now changing with re-evaluation of the role of diaconal ministry.

10  *An Anglican–Methodist Covenant*, p. 61 (Affirmation no. 7).

episcopacy as a form of church government; indeed, some, most prominently Hugh Price Hughes (1847–1902), even commended its missionary potential in the pre-ecumenical era. To the end of his life, and despite his many anguished questions about the *practical* effectiveness of the empirically existing system of oversight within the Church of England of his days, Wesley continued to believe that the threefold ministry was the most ancient and venerable system within Christendom.

Methodists who have been doubtful about the value of episcopacy have sometimes quoted a statement of Wesley's to the effect that the 'unbroken succession from the apostles is a fable that no man ever did or could prove', a statement he made after reading Lord Justice King's book on the subject in 1746. What King argued and Wesley took on board as a scholarly view has of course been accepted by modern scholars, including those from churches that insist on its value as a product of providential evolution within the second century. When Wesley, after nearly 40 years of vainly cajoling successive bishops of London to act in this matter, took upon himself, in 1784, to organize a church in the Americas for his converts, he gave that church a threefold ministry and then said that he was leaving it to the scriptures and the primitive church. [11]

However relative his view of the episcopal succession *per se* may have become, Wesley never doubted the supreme importance of *episcope* as such, and Methodism has always argued that it has safeguarded this whether with a separate order of bishops (as in the United States) or without, as to date, here in United Kingdom. It can even be argued that Wesley devised one of the most effective systems of *episcope* at a whole variety of levels, from that of the national Conference down to the immediate oversight of small groups by their 'class leaders'. While it is true that at many levels the Methodist emphasis has traditionally been on

---

11 For an account of Wesley's evolving views on the nature of the Christian ministry, see Albert Brown Lawson, *John Wesley and the Christian Ministry* (London: SPCK, 1963).

corporate, collegial oversight, most particularly that of the corporate body of presbyteral ministers over each other through the Annual Conferences, nevertheless, the individual oversight of superintendent ministers, ministers in pastoral charge and class leaders has been important. There is no reason why British Methodists should not look to the example of personal *episcope* exercised by bishops, both in their own sister Methodist churches and more widely, especially in those churches with which they already have relations of pulpit and altar fellowship,[12] or, as with the Churches of England and Ireland, a covenantal relationship.

Methodists have held in tension two truths: first, their conviction that it is possible for a true church to exist without the actual sign of the episcopal succession. In certain circumstances, churches have had to do without the sign of the episcopal succession. Examples include the Evangelical Church of Germany at the time of the Reformation when (unlike in Sweden) the bishops failed to safeguard the gospel of grace in their teaching. In the 1790s Methodism felt it had to break with Anglican order for the sake of its mission of evangelizing those areas of the country where the Anglican system was not sufficient. In Wesley's words, Methodists had to go 'not to those who need you, but to those who need you most'. The second truth (perhaps 'reality' is a better term) is that the majority of Christendom has always treasured the sign of the episcopal succession. As a matter of practical reality this has to be accepted. If one takes the call to unity seriously, then there has to be a very good reason for *not* being prepared to re-receive that sign, however important it may have been for some churches in very different historic circumstances to depart from it in earlier ages.[13]

---

12  As, for example, with the churches of Norway and Sweden, the former also through membership of the former Leuenberg Agreement (now the Community of European Protestant Churches).

13  I have also urged this as a consideration upon the German Evangelical Church where there is still widespread reluctance to consider re-receiving the sign of the episcopal succession, although

In the early years of the Faith and Order movement, Methodists recognized that the coming Great Church would have episcopal, presbyteral and congregational elements within its polity. Methodism was the one free church to respond positively to Archbishop Fisher's invitation to consider taking episcopacy into its system. Subsequently, the Methodist Conference twice approved a unity scheme that, had it also achieved the requisite Anglican vote, would have involved British Methodism in having bishops. In the subsequent abortive covenanting scheme of the 1970s, Methodism once again approved a scheme for covenanting with the Church of England, the United Reformed Church and the Moravians that would have involved Methodism in receiving bishops. On this second occasion, the Methodist Faith and Order committee, at the behest of Conference, devoted considerable energy to examining the question of how Methodist bishops should be selected and function.[14]

In its response to the *Baptism, Eucharist, Ministry* (BEM)[15] process of the World Council of Churches' Faith and Order Committee, British Methodism said that 'we await the moment for the recovery of the sign of the episcopal succession'.[16] The emphasis within that process upon the sign of the episcopal succession as 'sign but not guarantee' was helpful to the debate within Methodism, as was its reaffirmation in the Porvoo agreement. This means that Methodists are not bound to accept any understanding of the inerrancy of the episcopate as a whole, whilst being open to recognize the very real value of the sign of the succession and the value of the episcopate as a focus of communion across space and time.

---

the 'post-Meissen' situation is admittedly totally different from that of the sixteenth century.

14  For the details of this, see *Statements*, Vol. 1, pp. 204–35.

15  *Baptism, Eucharist and Ministry* (Geneva: World Council of Churches, 1982).

16  Max Thurian, *Churches Respond to BEM* (Geneva: WCC, 1985), Vol. 2, p. 215.

It has to be admitted that many Methodists, strong as may be their geographical connexional sense that 'the Methodist people are one people the world over', do not have as strong a sense of connexionalism across time, even though such an understanding is implicit within the Methodist tradition in the hymns of Charles Wesley and elsewhere.[17] I have, admittedly rather exaggeratedly, sometimes caricatured the popular Methodist understanding of church history as intermittently episodic rather than continuous, the key episodes being the Acts of the Apostles, the era of the Wesleys and their own times, with maybe the Reformation or other episodes mercifully intervening. There is not the *overall* sense of Christian history that tends to exist in churches that cherish the episcopal succession. To my mind – which I admit is not here necessarily typical of modern Methodist thinking – one of the gains in receiving the sign of the episcopal succession would be a heightened awareness of the continuity of the Church as a whole, and a deeper desire to explore the heritage of every age, even those that have had their striking failures.

At the official theological level, Methodism has, in recent years, devoted much attention to the question of episcopacy. In the year 2000, the Conference produced its statement on *episcope* and episcopacy.[18] I was a member of the working party that produced the draft report. We started with a very detailed examination of our current structures of *episcope* with particular reference to the classification of *episcope* within the BEM documents as personal, collegial, and communal. This investigation raised a whole raft of questions about its exercise. Recognizing the diversity of models of episcopacy within the worldwide Church, a section of the report was devoted to examining these models; we took note, in

---

17  See e.g. *Hymns and Psalms* (the official current Methodist hymnal), nos 752–63. For a theological account, see also W. F. Slater, *Methodism in the Light of the Early Church* (London: Woolmer, 1885).

18  *Statements of the Methodist Church on Faith and Order* (Peterborough: Epworth Press, 2000), Vol. 2, pp. 409–10.

particular, of the different styles of episcopacy within the three separate Anglican churches of mainland Britain.

Finally, we produced a summary of the conditions under which we felt that Methodism might receive the sign of the episcopal succession. It was made clear that Methodism was a connexional church and that 'all *episcope* should be exercised within this context'. The paramount role of mission was stressed: 'Methodists believe that a key function of *episcope* is to enable and encourage the Church's participation in mission.' It is worth mentioning in this context that the early American Methodist bishops were, above all, mission pioneers and enablers, assigning the elders to their frontier circuits and constantly travelling with and amongst them to share in their labour and to encourage them. A mission-leading role was stressed in the proposals to the Conference of 2005 referred to above.[19]

The specific conditions for the receipt of the sign of the episcopal succession are worth reflecting upon within an ecumenical context. It was made clear that Methodism would be unable to receive the sign if in any way that reception were 'to involve a repudiation of what the Methodist Church believed itself to have received from God'. It would be important for any ecumenical partner sharing the sign with the Methodist Church 'to acknowledge that the latter has been and is part of the One Holy Catholic and Apostolic Church'.

The two other key considerations are as follows:

> The Methodist Church, in contemplating the possibility of receiving the sign of the historic episcopal succession, expects to engage in dialogue with its sister churches to clarify as thoroughly as possible the nature and benefits of this gift.

> The Methodist Church, in receiving the sign of the episcopal succession, would insist that all ministries,

---

19  See above, n. 1.

including those of oversight, are exercised within the
ministry of the whole people of God and at its service,
rather than in isolation from it and in supremacy over it.

The first of these is obviously a mutual duty in any reception
process. It is important that in any ecumenical exchange of gifts
both 'giving' churches and 'receiving' churches understand how
the apostolicity and catholicity of the Church are being enhanced
in the process. The second consideration should create no
problems within the currently developing ecumenical ecclesiological consensus upon the Church as communion (*koinonia*). The
French Dominican ecclesiologist, Jean-Marie Tillard, constantly
emphasized the bishop as the one who listens to the voice of his
local church and relays its insights and concerns to the rest of the
Church. He is the focus of unity, the one who acts with his
presbyters and his laypeople, not simply by his own initiative. He
– and here we should wish also to add 'or she' – represents the
universal in the local and the local in the universal.[20] The
definition of the government of the Church of England given in
the *Called to Be One* process of Churches Together in England in
the 1990s, namely, that the Church is 'synodically governed but
episcopally led', comes close to what would be acceptable in
Methodism where the Conference, which contains representative
presbyters, deacons and laypeople (and would presumably include
bishops as well), would continue to *govern* but would expect good
*leadership*, with a particular emphasis upon mission, from any
Methodist bishops.

The reference at the end of the second condition to 'isolation'
and 'supremacy' was probably included out of deference to
continuing fears amongst some Methodists of bishops as 'proud
prelates'. Prejudices entertained within a particular denomination
about another often reflect past rather than current situations.

---

20  For the fullest account of his theology of the relationship of bishop
and local and universal Church, see his *L'Église locale: ecclésiologie de
communion et catholicité* (Paris: Cerf, 1995).

Some Methodists have not caught up with the fact that Bishop
Jim or Mike is usually just that, rather than the 'My Lord' of 50
years ago. However, it will be important for Anglicans to honour
the flexibility of the expression 'the historic episcopate, locally
adapted'. One felt this was lacking when the Church in Wales
failed to approve the ecumenical bishop scheme, arguing *inter alia*,
that the call for a bishop to serve for a limited term did not fit the
criteria. One remembers not merely that most Anglican bishops
now retire but that it is certainly not unknown for a bishop to
move into a role that is not *per se* episcopal, the recently retired
Dean of Liverpool, the Rt Revd Rupert Hoare being an example
of this.

Methodism will, of course, have to make decisions about who
should be appointed bishop. It might seem obvious to non-
Methodists that the chairs of districts, who sometimes cover
similar areas and certainly often relate closely to the Anglican
diocesans within their districts, would be the obvious choices.
Recently, in an exercise designed to refine its whole understanding of the three different ministries, Methodism has
produced a report entitled *What is a Bishop?*, where the question of
whether it should be the successive presidents of Conference who
become bishops or the chairs of districts, or even possibly the
superintendent ministers, has been raised.

Historically, it is the case that the superintendents of circuits
have been those who have exercised the most far-reaching
personal *episcope*. The role of the chairs of districts was far more
limited and, in fact, until the 1950s, this was well indicated by
their historic title 'chairman of the district synod'. In recent years,
however, the role of the chairs in active *episcope* has become much
more pronounced. In particular, they now play a key role in the
whole process of stationing ministers. To make all superintendents bishops, at least if circuits of the present normal size
were retained, would mean creating a British Methodist
episcopate of several hundred. Nevertheless, the case for having
bishops with oversight of areas smaller than our present districts,

even if considerably bigger than most circuits, is not negligible.[21] It is a case with which many Anglicans, who point to the historically small size of dioceses in the Early Church and also to the pastoral advantages for the present of smaller ones, might sympathize. Bishops with smaller dioceses would be able to know their clergy and many of their lay leaders far better.

Very recently, and largely since the publication of *What Sort of Bishops?*, Methodism has begun to consider the possibility of larger circuits with perhaps three dozen or so congregations served by a dozen or more presbyters, rather than the present smaller circuits with a dozen or so churches and four to six presbyters. It would be a pity if this suggestion could not be fed into the Methodist discussion of episcopacy since such enlarged circuits might prove ideal episcopal units.[22]

In 2007 the Methodist Conference was due to debate the report *What Sort of Bishops?* and decide whether there should be Methodist bishops and, if so, of what sort. The report had already been commended for study and response by the districts and circuits. However, due to the lack of enthusiasm shown for the proposals in most of the responses, the Methodist Council decided that it would not be opportune to proceed to the debate, though it accepted that the existence of the Covenant and the commitments within it meant that the matter would eventually be bound to resurface.[23]

There is, nevertheless, little doubt in my mind that support for a Methodist episcopate, particularly amongst women presbyters and lay women, would be reinforced by an indication that the

---

21 One of the recommendations in the 2005 report is, in fact, along these lines.

22 Very recently, it has been decided that the five circuits covering the administrative areas of the city and county of Bristol and of South Gloucestershire unitary authority should be amalgamated, in 2008, as one circuit with 60 worshipping congregations.

23 The Methodist Council carries out a role within Methodism similar to that of the Archbishops' Council within the Church of England.

Church of England is likely to admit women to the episcopate, particularly if this is done without too many longer-term concessions to the opponents of such a move. Many Methodist women feel strongly about the issue, and it is to be noted that the Methodist Conference felt able to resume negotiations for a closer relationship with the Church of England in 1994 only after the definitive decision to admit women to the priesthood.[24]

## Concluding Reflections

I return finally to a few reflections on the subject in the light of the Methodist theological tradition. The classical Wesleyan tradition regarded the pastoral office as being of divine institution within the Church, with a responsibility for the ministry of the word and sacraments and for general oversight. It did not believe that it had to take either an invariably episcopal or presbyteral form. It also accepted that, on occasion, circumstances might dictate a break in ministerial succession, whether this was determined by the unfaithfulness of existing pastors or the need, as in America in 1784, for an urgent initiative that was not forthcoming from the traditional sources. It was accepted that while the ministry of the 'under-shepherds to the Great Shepherd' must be preserved in the Church, forms of church life also have to be able to be adapted, such adaptability being not merely legitimate but, on occasion, necessary.[25]

This adaptability would seem to be demanded both by a recovery of the apostolic tradition that women did indeed hold some leadership roles within the Early Church – one thinks of Junia, ranked among the apostles (Rom. 16.7) and of the many women leaders to whom Paul refers – and by the greatly altered

---

24  By the same token, any synodical vote rejecting a proposal to admit women to the episcopate would certainly have a negative effect on the developing relationship with in the Covenant.

25  Benjamin Gregory, *Handbook of Scriptural Church Principles and of Wesleyan–Methodist Polity and History* (London: Wesleyan–Methodist Book Room, 1888), p. 90.

condition of women in twentieth-century society. Not so long ago, it was assumed that women were by nature not fitted to discharge highly responsible professional roles. A doctor even protested against the teaching of such subjects as mathematics and classics to girls in the first real secondary schools established for them in the nineteenth century, on the grounds that their brains would not be able to cope with the intellectual strain. Generations of scholarly and competent professional women have since proved the absurdity of such ideas.

In recent years, some conservative Roman Catholic scholars, attempting to give an anthropological rationale for the repeated insistence of both Paul VI and John Paul II that the Catholic Church cannot alter the rules concerning the non-ordination of women, have argued that men and women have naturally different spiritual vocations and that, in particular, women cannot represent Christ in his headship, even though they can represent him in other ways as baptized Christians. Such speculative ideas seem to Methodists to lack the biblical support which does exist for the inclusiveness of the Church, in which there is neither Greek nor Jew, slave nor free, male nor female. They also seem disputable in terms of actual experience where women are discharging all the initiating and leadership aspects of the pastoral office and, arguably, adding a richness of approach through their qualities. It also seems questionable, in view of the uniqueness of the creation of each person, to argue that certain spiritual capacities, as opposed to purely biological characteristics, are confined to one sex rather than the other.

At a recent synod, the Bishop of Bristol, Mike Hill, reminded his synod that the Church of England is a reformed branch of the Catholic Church and, as such, claims the right to carry our reforms and changes that enhance its life and witness without breaking essential principles of apostolic faith and practice. Both the Church of England and the Methodist Church are at one in this understanding of reformed catholicity.[26] Both accept that important changes were needed in the sixteenth century and that these were made in conscious fidelity to the faith once delivered to the saints. The further changes in early Methodism were made in the same spirit and with the same goal.

In this connection, I remember the wisdom of a very senior Methodist minister of yesteryear who told me, in the mid-1970s, that although he certainly believed there were women with the gifts and graces for the work, he did not expect women ever to form more than a small proportion of the ministry. At that stage there were, of course, far fewer women at the top of the key professions than there are today, and it was perhaps natural to make such an assumption. I suspect that, were he alive today, he would gladly revise his view. The fact is that for both Methodists and Anglicans neither church could survive pastorally without women presbyters. Even if they could, both churches would be spiritually the poorer without the insights that women have brought to presbyteral ministry. I think we may be confident that if women have enriched the practice of presbyteral ministry, the same would be true of the episcopate.

---

26 Canon A1 talks of the Church of England as 'part of the one holy, catholic church' and the Deed of Union talks of Methodism claiming and cherishing its place within the one holy Catholic Church. Both churches have maintained the use of the word 'catholic' as against the example of some continental Protestant churches that have relinquished the term in favour of 'universal', which is not an exact equivalent.

# 6

## Episcopal–Synodical Church Structure: Some Reflections on Issues of Synodality and Authority from an Old Catholic Perspective[1]

ANGELA BERLIS

### Authority in the Old Catholic Churches

This chapter offers some fundamental reflections on episcopal–synodical church structure, important when considering authority as authority in dialogue: for unity is based upon authority in dialogue. This is an ancient model as has been noted by the Swiss Old Catholic bishop, Urs Küry: 'The early church was constituted according to episcopal–synodical principles.'[2] Episcopal–synodical structures can be found in the New Testament ordering of the congregation (particularly in Acts and in the Pastoral Epistles) and became well established towards the end of the second century. In this, as in many other aspects of its theology and life, the Early Church is the primary guide and measure for the Old Catholic Church.[3]

---

1    This chapter is adapted from Angela Berlis, 'Episcopal–Synodical Church Structure and Authority in Dialogue', in Jan Hallebeek (ed.), *Gezag als gave. Gezag in de kerk in oecumenisch spanningsveld* (Publicatieserie Stichting Oud-Katholiek Seminarie 37, Amersfoort-Sliedrecht: Merweboek, 2004), pp. 55–79.

2    Urs Küry, *Die Altkatholische Kirche. Ihre Geschichte, ihre Lehre, ihr Anliegen*. References to the second edition edited by Christian Oeyen (Stuttgart: Evangelisches Verlagswerk, 1978), p. 17.

3    For the history and structure of the Old Catholic Churches, see Urs von Arx, 'The Old Catholic Churches of the Union of Utrecht', in Paul Avis (ed.), *The Christian Church. An Introduction to the Major Traditions* (London: SPCK, 2002), pp. 157–85; Jan Visser, 'The Old

62

Questions about authority in the Church became particularly important to Catholics during the nineteenth century.[4] The experience of the dogmatizing of papal infallibility and jurisdictional primacy in 1870, and the way in which these new dogmas were 'planted' in the dioceses (here one should avoid speaking of 'reception') led to the founding of the Old Catholic movement in several German-speaking countries and prompted Old Catholics to consider their own understanding of authority in the Church.[5] The discussions at the earliest Old Catholic congresses of 1871–73 reflect a deep disappointment with bishops who had gradually given in to Rome over the new dogmas, and the hope of renewal in the office of bishop according to the model of the Early Church. There was a strong Anglican presence even at these early congresses,[6] indicating an ecumenical interest which culminated in the Bonn Agreement of 1931, in which Anglicans and Old Catholics entered into a relationship of communion.

Against the new Vatican dogmas, but according to Catholic teaching, the Old Catholics held that a bishop must exercise direct

Catholic Churches of the Union of Utrecht', in *International Journal for the Study of the Christian Church* 3 (2003), pp. 68–84.

4 For reasons of space, the schism between Rome and Utrecht (1723) and the development of thinking about church structure in the Old Catholic Church of the Netherlands cannot be discussed. This too was rooted in questions of authority. On this see John Mason Neale, *A History of the So-called Jansenist Church of Holland* (Oxford: Parker, 1858). For further literature, see above, nn. 1 and 3.

5 For the development of the Old Catholic movement from Vatican I until its development of independent structures, see Angela Berlis, *Frauen im Prozeß der Kirchwerdung. Eine historisch-theologische Studie zur Anfangsphase des deutschen Altkatholizismus (1850–1890)* (Frankfurt: Peter Lang, 1998), esp. ch. 1.

6 See for example the following Anglican accounts: James Lowry Whittle, *Catholicism and the Vatican. With a Narrative of the Old Catholic Congress at Munich* (London: King, 1872); Christopher Wordsworth, *Old Catholic Congress. A Letter from the Bishop of Lincoln on his Return from the Congress at Cologne* (Lincoln: Williamson, 1872).

and independent leadership in his diocese.[7] Overall ecclesiastical authority is vested, not in the pope alone, but in the whole College of Bishops. In his first pastoral letter of 1873, the German bishop Joseph Hubert Reinkens emphasized the importance of the *election* of bishops: 'In those days [the early Church], a bishop would never have been accepted as belonging to the college of *catholic* bishops unless he had been elected by the clergy and the people.'[8] The election of a bishop by his church is an important expression of the relationship between the local church and the bishop (elect).

The bishop is not to be understood as a sovereign. His office is to proclaim the good news and to be 'organizer and administrator of the sacraments' on behalf of the people.[9] In this view, Reinkens comes very close to the fundamental Dutch Old Catholic understanding that the bishop's authority and jurisdiction is rooted in and derived from the Church.[10]

At the same time, the Church is a community of both clergy and laity, and is not constituted only by those who hold office. A primary interest for the Old Catholics was to do away with the hierarchical distinction between clergy and laity and to see the Church rather as the 'people of God', sealed through the Holy Spirit in baptism. Since believers are the children of God, they

---

7    Nuremberg Declaration, 26 August 1870, point 4 and Programme of the Catholic Congress in Munich, 1871, point II. On this, see C. B. Moss, *The Old Catholic Movement, its Origins and History* (London: SPCK; 1964; 2nd edn), pp. 227–8 and 235.

8    Joseph Hubert Reinkens, *Hirtenbriefe* (Bonn: privately published 1897), p. 3. English trans. by George Edgar Broade and John Eyton Bickersteth Mayor: Bishop Reinkens, *First Pastoral Letter (11 August 1873) and Speech on Bible Reading* (London: privately published, 1874).

9    Reinkens, *Hirtenbriefe*, p. 16. Reinkens is here alluding to 1 Cor. 4.1.

10   See Jan Hallebeek, *Alonso 'El Tostado' (c. 1410–1455). His doctrine on jurisdiction and its influence in the Church of Utrecht* (Publicatieserie Stichting Oud-Katholiek Seminarie 29, Amersfoort Stichting Centraal Oud-Katholiek Boekhuis, 1997), esp. pp. 32–3.

have certain rights. The primary responsibility of the bishop is that of 'God's housekeeper', with ultimate responsibility shared by the whole Church. In the Old Catholic Church, this shared responsibility takes place through synodical structures which are anchored in canon law; it is greatly valued in the life of the individual churches.

The particular form of the episcopal–synodical structure of the Old Catholic Church differs from church to church, and the episcopal–synodical structure may be realized through a variety of structures and bodies. However, the principle that the bishop exercises his authority collegially and synodically within his diocese is common to all. The consequence of this is, for example, that bishops and dioceses who wish to join the Union of Utrecht can only be admitted if they have episcopal–synodical structures allowing both laity and clergy to be involved in the leadership and administration of the Church.[11]

In recent decades, awareness of the importance of synodality has also increased in ecumenical dialogues, as seen for instance in the ARCIC III report, *The Gift of Authority*.[12] In its report, the Dutch 'Joint Commission Rome–Utrecht', argues that 'most traditions are united in seeing the necessity of a synodical "context" for the exercise of episcopal office'. Bishops may not behave as autocrats, but are called to 'confer synodically with priests, deacons, and other representatives of the church and to confer collegially with their episcopal colleagues'. However, the report adds, 'the form of synodical conferring takes different forms and has different authority'. In appealing to synodality, the

11  See the 'Guidelines of the International Bishops' Conference (IBK) with Respect to the Recognition of a Church as Independent Old Catholic Church of the Utrecht Union', 27 June 2002 at:
   http://www.utrechter-union.org/english/ibc_documents003.htm
12  See *The Gift of Authority. Authority in the Church III. An Agreed Statement by the Anglican–Roman Catholic International Commission (ARCIC)* (Toronto: Anglican Book Centre, London: Catholic Truth Society, New York: Church Publishing, 1999), esp. §§34–40.

specific responsibility of the bishops for maintaining tradition and for the preservation of unity is not restricted.[13]

## Aspects of synodality

According to the Greek word from which it derives, synodality means 'to travel a road together'. A *synodos* may refer to a gathering, but also to a group of travellers. In the Acts of the Apostles, those who proclaim Jesus, crucified and resurrected, are referred to as 'the people of the (new) way' (Acts 9.2). Together these people of the way follow Christ, who is 'the Way' (Jn 14.6). In the New Testament, the term συνάγειν is used to refer both to the synod of the Apostles (Acts 15.6) and the gathering of the community to celebrate the eucharist (1 Cor. 5.4). In a similar way, the word 'ecclesia' indicates the combining of the synodical ordering of the Church with the Church's understanding of itself as a eucharistic community. One might argue that 'the synodality of the church arises from its essence as a eucharistic community'.[14]

In the New Testament there is frequent allusion to the double origin of the Church: on the one hand through the apostolic task given by the resurrected Christ; on the other through the filling of the whole community with the Spirit at Pentecost. These two principles are not exclusive, as is made clear by the Pauline image of the one body of Christ which has many members (1 Cor. 12).

---

13  *Het gezamenlijk erfgoed in vreugde delen. Advies aan het bestuur van de Katholieke Vereniging voor Oecumene inzake de verhouding tussen de Oud-Katholieke en de Rooms-Katholieke Kerk in Nederland*, no. 30. Available at: http://www.oecumene.nl/documenten/2004-01-29%20GezErf goedInVreugdeDelen.doc. Published in German in *Internationale Kirchliche Zeitschrift* (hereafter *IKZ*) 94 (2004), pp. 249–76.

14  Theodor Nikolaou, 'Zur Synodalität der Kirche. Kirchengeschichtliche Betrachtungen', in Gunther Wenz (ed.), *Ekklesiologie und Kirchenverfassung. Die institutionelle Gestalt des episkopalen Dienstes* (Münster: Lit, 2003), pp. 43–62, here p. 48.

The apostolic task and the responsibility of leadership which arises from it are both a part of the body of Christ.

At the Munich (Old) Catholic Congress of 1871, Johannes Huber, Professor of Philosophy in Munich, drew on this Pauline image. His interpretation was shaped by the polemical conflict around the First Vatican Council and the contemporary context of the industrial revolution. Huber suggested:

> Whatever the Church is, she must be it also as a result of the inward involvement of all its members. The Church, unlike a machine, should not be set in motion by *one* hand and sent in a particular direction; instead, the Church builds itself organically from the living and creative power of Christian teaching which is present in every member of the Church.[15]

Synodality begins with the shared action of the whole people of God: of laity and clergy, of theologians and bishop(s). The Church lives and grows as a result of the interplay between clergy and laity and their shared responsibility.

The soil in which synodality can grow, be learned and lived is the congregation. As the German Old Catholic Bishop Joachim Vobbe has written: 'The foundation for synodical life is the "creation of Christian community" that is, the community of self-aware, engaged, active Christians living together in fellowship.'[16] Synodality assumes maturity and responsibility. This is not simply a matter of knowing one's rights and responsibilities; nor is it only a matter of applying one's own expertise in questions of conscience or within one's own sphere of knowledge. Synodality

---

15  *Stenographischer Bericht über die Verhandlungen des Katholiken-Congresses abgehalten vom 22. bis 24 September 1871 in München. Mit einer historischen Einleitung und Beilagen* (Munich: Ackermann, 1871), p. 7.

16  Joachim Vobbe, 'Theodor Stumpf aus Koblenz – ein Cusanus-Verehrer an der Wiege der alt-katholischen Synodal- und Gemeindeordnung', in *IKZ* 93 (2003), pp. 65–82, here p. 82.

is a matter of bearing responsibility and sharing in the implementation of decisions made in synodical consensus.

In the Old Catholic Church, synodality is expressed in the shared process of decision-making in conversation and prayer together. But synodality is not only about action; it is an attitude, rooted in the knowledge that we are always journeying together. It assumes a critical awareness of power, and it is therefore important that structures allow minorities and the views of minorities to be articulated and heard. Decision-making is not a question of finding a simple majority, but of finding a consensus which is based on a common mind and which will thus be widely supported. This latter aspect is important if decisions made by the bishop and synod are to be implemented – received – in the life of the Church.

This means that synodality requires a distinction to be drawn between 'power' and 'authority'. Authority is not gained automatically through ecclesiastical office, but by those who recognize and accept that authority. The election of a particular person as a bishop or as a member of a committee or other body in the Church is not only the expression of trust but also the according of authority to that person. Without this authority, a person cannot fulfil the duties of his or her office, but this authority also delineates that office. This is not a question of *absolute* freedom of action, but of action and authority granted by the Church in a synodical way and of responsibility held in accordance with that authority. Authority and power are thus held in balance and are exercised with accountability.

Synodality assumes leadership structures which understand leadership in terms of service: as listening, with speech and action based upon what has been heard. If church leadership is understood in this way, it will offer the treasures of the tradition to believers in such a way as to take seriously the experiences and the lives of people today. This means that in the Old Catholic Church authority is exercised in dialogue, or in reciprocity. Authority is primarily interpersonal and reciprocal, formed by human encounters in partnership. This aspect must not be lost even in the 'higher' echelons of the Church. Institutionally anchored authority is partly dependent on the ability of the office-holder to convince. Such a view of synodality assumes the personal exercise of authority and responsibility. In the Old Catholic view, *episkope* is best exercised in this personal dimension, that is, personally, by real individuals, rather than through a committee or another institutional body. *Episkope* should therefore be understood less in terms of 'oversight' and rather as the 'exercising of primary responsibility'.[17]

Synodality is exercised and realized at many different levels within the Church, from the local congregation to diocesan or provincial level (for instance by the consecration of a new bishop by the neighbouring bishops). Ultimately, synodality is the basis of internal and external ecumenism – the external representation of the local church by its bishop was an early development. The bishop is accordingly responsible both to his diocese and to the wider Church. This includes not only the Church in all places, but also the Church at all times, as is symbolized by the doctrine of apostolic succession. It is the task of the bishops to keep in mind the needs of the local church in the context of the whole church in all times and all places. This is sometimes a difficult balancing act, for the bishop must seek to be fair to all and have a good sense of what is possible and what is necessary, whilst also bearing the *primary* responsibility in his local church for the preservation of the unity of the whole Church. This final level of synodality is best realized in an ecumenical council. But although there is unlikely to be such a council in the foreseeable future, it is

17  Urs von Arx translates *episkope* as 'Erstverantwortung', which has here been rendered as 'primary responsibility'. See Urs von Arx, 'Identity, Pluarality, Unity – What's the Right Blend? Some Reflections from an Old Catholic Perspective', in Jeremy Morris and Nicholas Sagovsky (eds), *The Unity We Have and the Unity We Seek. Ecumenical Prospects for the Third Millennium* (London: T&T Clark, 2003), pp. 3–26, here p. 18. His ideas are based upon the work of the Swiss Old Catholic New Testament exegete and theologian Kurt Stalder.

nevertheless our task to practise 'conciliarity' and conciliar living together.

The Union of Utrecht offers one means of making visible the community and communion of the local churches. The union binds together the Old Catholic bishops and their churches. The preamble to the Statutes of the International Old Catholic Bishops' Conference (IBC) formulates it thus:

> [The bishops] stand at the intersection of primarily belonging, as individuals, to their local or national church on the one hand, and of taking, as a college, primary responsibility for the fellowship and communion of the local and national churches on the other hand.[18]

An Old Catholic bishop represents his church, which he leads synodically and collegially, to his fellow bishops in the International Bishops' Conference, while to his church he represents the communion of the Union of Utrecht, of which he is collegially and synodically a part. From its beginning, the Old Catholic Bishops' Conference has been understood as a synodical body, in which the views of local churches are expressed through their bishop.[19] The Orthodox theologian Theodor Nikolaou sees the representation of local churches by their bishops as 'probably the most important "democratic element" in the synodical ordering of the church', for this representation preserves not only the collegiality and equality of the bishops, but also the independence of the local churches.[20]

---

18  Statute of the Old Catholic Bishops United in the Union of Utrecht, A, no. 4, in Supplement to *IKZ* 9 (2001), p. 30.

19  This does not mean that the IBC is an ecumenical or provincial council. The legal character of the IBC is instead comparable to provincial conferences of bishops. See Jan Hallebeek, 'Canon Law Aspects of the Utrecht Union', in *IKZ* 84 (1994), pp. 114–27.

20  Nikolaou, 'Zur Synodalität der Kirche', p. 50.

The episcopal–synodical structures as they are lived in the Old Catholic Churches of the Union of Utrecht thus shed light on the way in which community and leadership exist in terms of shared responsibility, authority in dialogue and even dissent.

# 7

# Women with Oversight: Evidence from the Early Church

CHARLOTTE METHUEN

If you will, traveller, note this inscription: "here lies the venerable lady, bishop Q—, laid to rest in peace"[1]

This sixth-century Umbrian inscription marks the tomb of an 'venerable lady, bishop Q—'. It is generally interpreted as referring to the wife of a bishop. However, as it survives, the inscription mentions neither a husband nor a male bishop. Moreover, the accolade *venerabilis* is generally accorded only to members of the clergy.[2] The inscription raises questions. Who was this 'venerable lady, bishop Q—'? What was her role?

---

1   'Si uis cog[n]o[sce, uia]tor: hic requie[scit] venerabilis fem[ina] episcopa Q .... depos. in pace ...' (inscription in Umbria, Italy, cited by Ute E. Eisen, *Amtsträgerinnen im frühen Christentum* (Göttingen: Vandenhoeck & Ruprecht, 1996), p. 193; trans. *Women Officeholders in Early Christianity: Epigraphical and Literary Studies* (Collegeville, MN: Liturgical Press, 2000). This chapter is an emended version of 'Vidua–Presbytera–Episcopa: Women with Oversight in the Early Church', in *Theology* 108 (2005), pp. 163–77, which in turn was an expanded version of 'Women with Oversight: Evidence from Scripture and Tradition', printed as a WATCH Occasional Paper in Spring 2004. It draws heavily on an earlier article published in German: Charlotte Methuen, 'Die Autorität von Frauen in der Alten Kirche am Beispiel der Syrischen Didascalia', in Leonore Siegele-Wenschkewitz and Gury Schneider-Ludorff *et al.* (eds), *Frauen Gestalten Geschichte* (Wiesbaden: Lutherisches Verlagshaus, 1998), pp. 9–32.

2   Eisen, *Amtsträgerinnen*, p. 194.

A Latin epitaph from the cemetery of the Basilica of Saint Valentinae commemorates 'the honourable lady, bishop'.[3] Who was she?

A mosaic in the Zeno chapel of St Prassede in Rome dating to the ninth century shows four women. Three (Mary and the Saints Praxedis and Prudentiana) have their heads highlighted by the round golden halos of saints; one has her head enclosed in the square white halo which traditionally indicated the portrait of a living person, honoured or regarded as holy. In the mosaic, this figure bears the title 'Theodora Episcopa'. An inscription on a reliquary in the same chapel records the donation of relics by Pope Paschal I to the chapel, the resting-place 'of his most good mother, namely the lady Theodora, Bishop'.[4] Like that of the 'venerable lady, bishop Q—', and the entirely anonymous 'honourable lady, bishop', Theodora's title has been interpreted variously. Was she named bishop in recognition of the position of her son, the pope? Was she a supervisor or overseer of virgins and widows, or the equivalent of an abbess? Or had she perhaps been ordained bishop?[5]

It is probably impossible to be certain of the correct interpretation of these inscriptions. Scholars often interpret these inscriptions and others referring to women as priests, presbyters or stewards as honorific: as pointing to a close relationship between the woman and a man who held that office. The 'venerable lady,

3   '[Hono]rabilis femina episcopa', cited by Joan Morris, *Against Nature and God: The History of Women with Clerical Ordination and the Jurisdiction of Bishops* (Oxford: Mowbray, 1973), p. 6. Also published as *The Lady was a Bishop: The Hidden History of Women with Clerical Ordination and the Jurisdiction of Bishops* (New York and London: Macmillan, 1973).
4   Cited by Eisen, *Amtsträgerinnen*, pp. 195–6; cf. Morris, *Against Nature and God*, pp. 4–6. See also Karen Jo Torjesen, *When Women were Priests: Women's Leadership in the Early Church and the Scandal of their Subordination in the Rise of Christianity* (San Francisco, CA: HarperCollins, 1995), pp. 9–10.
5   Eisen, *Amtsträgerinnen*, pp. 199–201.

bishop Q—' is then not the memorial of a woman who was a bishop in her own right, but of the wife of a bishop, that is 'Mrs Bishop', or (in the German usage common in the later nineteenth century and first half of the twentieth) 'Frau Bischof'. This may say as much, if not more, more about an interpreter's expectations than about the woman herself. If a scholar encounters such an inscription, or a text which uses such titles of women, but 'knows' that the Church has never allowed women to take those sorts of roles, then that scholar will not attribute those roles to those women and will seek another explanation of the title.

Jean Daniélou, a meticulous scholar of the Early Church, translated all incidences of *presbytera* – the feminine form of presbyter – as widow. As will be demonstrated later, there were grounds for this translation, since in the Early Church the term widow could also be a title for women ministers. However, for those who do not recognize 'widow' as a title – and a highly honoured title at that – such translations serve rather to disguise the fact that titles – and indeed ministerial titles – are being used of these women. A scholar who does not believe that women can have such titles will not even envision the possibility. On the other hand, a scholar who assumes that it is possible that women did play a role in the ministry and oversight of the Early Church finds an extraordinary range of sources which indicate both the existence of such ministries but also the protracted struggle to prevent them.

This chapter will sketch briefly some of that evidence, and the problems of its interpretation, before considering how this evidence might be relevant to the current debates in the Church of England.

**Bishops and episcopal leadership in the New Testament**

Both episcopacy and the threefold ministry result from a long and complex history of development. The office of bishop, scarcely mentioned in the New Testament, gained enormously in importance in the second and third centuries until in the course of the fourth and fifth centuries it became central to the dominant structure of the Church.[6] There are very few New Testament references either to the office of *episcope* or to the holder of that office, an *episcopos*: Phil. 1.1; Acts 20.28; 1 Tim. 3.1–2; Tit. 1.7 (and to Christ as *episcopos* in 1 Pet.). These brief allusions give little clue to the function of the people to which they refer. Inscriptions and non-biblical writings suggest that the term *episcopos* generally referred to an administrator or overseer: an interpretation which is often reflected in a number of English translations of these passages. Moreover, at this stage terms such as *presbyteros* and *episcopos*, which later came to refer to distinctive roles and offices, were looser, and several titles could be applied to the same person or group of people. As Rebecca Lyman points out, 'the titles themselves are both functional and descriptive, i.e. the "sender of the gospel" (apostle) or "overseer" (bishop) or "elder/senior" (presbyter)'; all of these, together with 'patron' and 'widow', had a range of interpretations reflecting either a person's particular role or their social status within a community, or both.[7]

6   See most recently Francis A. Sullivan SJ, *From Apostles to Bishops: The Development of the Episcopate in the Early Church* (New York: Newman Press, 2001). The classic discussion is Hans von Campenhausen, *Ecclesiastical Authority and Spiritual Power in the Church of the First Three Centuries* (London: A. & C. Black, 1969). For a summary of the (extensive) scholarship, see Harry O. Maier, *The Social Setting of the Ministry as Reflected in the Writings of Hermas, Clement and Ignatius* (Waterloo, ON: Wilfrid Laurier University Press, 1991). Discussions in the Church of England tend to miss the complexity of these developments and the co-existence of different forms of leadership structures. See, for instance, *Women Bishops in the Church of England?* (London: Church House Publishing, 2004), pp. 9–26; and compare also Jonathan Baker (ed.), *Consecrated Women? A Contribution to the Women Bishops Debate* (Norwich: Canterbury Press with Forward in Faith, 2004), pp. 59–73.

7   Rebecca Lyman, 'Women Bishops in Antiquity: Apostolicity and Ministry', in Harriet Harris and Jane Shaw (eds), *The Call for Women Bishops* (London: SPCK, 2004), pp. 37–50, here p. 38.

There was little or no consistent structure across the emerging Christian communities.

## Women as apostles

The New Testament witnesses to a time of mission, in which local congregations and churches were being formed in response to the preaching of apostles. The New Testament term 'apostle' refers not only to the twelve and Paul, Barnabas and Timothy, but also to the woman Junia, who together with Andronicus is described by Paul as 'prominent amongst the apostles' (Rom. 16.7). John Chrysostom comments of Paul's greeting: 'How great is the wisdom of this woman, that she should be even counted worthy of the appellation of apostle!'[8] Junia is only one of a list of women whom Paul greets by name: the minister and benefactor Phoebe (of whom more later), Prisca with her partner Aquila, Mary, Tryphaena, Tryphosa, Persis, Julia and Olympa (Rom. 16.1-16). Reflecting on the greeting to Mary Rom. 16.6), Chrysostom concludes that this list of favoured women witnesses to their active ministry in Paul's time:

> How is this? A woman again is honoured and proclaimed victorious! Again are we men put to shame. Or rather, we are not put to shame only, but have even an honour conferred upon us. For an honour we have, in that there are such women amongst us, but we are put to shame, in that we men are left so far behind by them. ... For the women of those days were more spirited than lions, sharing with the Apostles their labours for the Gospel's sake. In this way they went travelling with them, and also performed all other ministries. And even in Christ's day there followed Him women, 'which ministered unto Him

---

8    John Chrysostom, homilia in epistolam Paulini ad Romanos (hom. ep. Paul. ad Rom.), 31.

of their substance' (Luke 8.3), and waited upon the
Teacher.[9]

Chrysostom, dismayed by the women of his own church, whom
he criticizes for being interested only in clothes and make-up,
rejoices over the spirit of the women known to Paul, who
'performed all ministries', and not only that of apostle.

Like Chysostom, Origen[10] and Jerome[11] also highlight Junia as
a female apostle. The patristic evidence is clear. However, writing
in the thirteenth century, Aegidus [Giles] of Rome argued that it
was impossible for a woman to be an apostle, so that Paul's
apparent reference to Junia must in fact be to Junias, a man.[12]
Many early-modern and modern Bible translations (not the AV,
but including the RSV) and even the Nestlé–Aland edition of the
Greek New Testament have followed Giles of Rome in making
the female Junia into Junias, a man. The NRSV corrects its
reading to Junia, as too does the Nestlé-Aland Jubilee edition.[13]
Most recently, in *Consecrated Women?* great emphasis has been laid

9    Hom. Ep. Paul. ad Rom., 31.
10   Origen, epistula ad Romanos commentaria, 10,23; 29.
11   Jerome, liber interpretationis hebraicum nominum, 72,15.
12   For the transformation to Junia into Junias and a summary of the
     literature pertaining to the translation of Rom 16.7, see Bernadette
     Brooten, 'Junia... Outstanding among the Apostles', in Leonard and
     Arlene Swidler (eds), *Women Priests: A Catholic Commentary on the
     Vatican Declaration* (New York: Paulist Press, 1977), pp. 141–4;
     Eisen, *Amtsträgerinnen*, pp. 50–55; Dianne D. McDonnell, 'Junia: A
     Woman Apostle', available at: http://www.churchofgoddfw.com/
     monthly/junia.shtml. Most recently, see Eldon Jay Epp, *Junia: The
     First Woman Apostle* (Minneapolis, MN: Fortress Press, 2005). For a
     detailed discussion of the semantics of the name and the lack of
     evidence for 'Junias', see John Thorley, 'Junia, a Woman Apostle',
     in *Novum Testamentum* 38 (1996), pp. 18–29, with further literature
     on the patristic tradition at n. 28.
13   For a precise discussion of the Greek, see Epp, *Junia* and Thorley,
     'Junia, a Woman Apostle'.

on the office of apostle as the origin of the office of bishop, and the NRSV's patristic correction has been criticized as a neologism: between the RSV and the NRSV, the authors suggest, 'a male *known to the apostles* has become a *famous female apostle!*'[14] This comment is doubly inept: firstly, because it favours the inferior translation of *episēmoi en tois apostolois* as 'known to the apostles', rather than as 'of note amongst the apostles', but also – and more importantly – in its misleading implication that the correction of Junias to Junia is an 'innovation' rather than a return to the original text as witnessed by the Fathers.

In considering the evidence for female apostles, it should be noted that the Samaritan woman (Jn 4.5–30), Mary Magdalen and the other women at the tomb were often referred to as apostles by early Christians (including Origen and Hippolytus of Rome),[15] and that Mary Magdalen and Thecla are honoured in Byzantine liturgy as 'equal to the apostles'. Thecla, a fellow apostle with Paul, rejected his suggestion that she was too beautiful to keep the faith and should marry instead, baptizing herself to show her dedication.[16] For many centuries she was more widely honoured in the Eastern Church than Mary,[17] and the Acts of Paul and Thecla were regarded by some parts of the Church as canonical until into the sixth century. There is an ancient and well-founded tradition which recognizes the apostleship of women.

---

14  *Consecrated Women?*, p. 65; italics in the original.

15  See Eisen, *Amtsträgerinnen*, pp. 59–64. The Byzantine liturgy honours Junia as an apostle, and Mary Magdalen and Thecla as 'equal to the apostles' (p. 52). For Mary Magdalen as an apostle, see also Ann Graham Brock, *Mary Magdalene, The First Apostle: The Struggle for Authority* (Cambridge, MA: Harvard Divinity School, 2003); and Silke Petersen, *'Zerstört die Werke der Weiblichkeit!': Maria Magdalena, Salome und andere Jüngerinnen Jesu in christlich-gnostischen Schriften* (Leiden: Brill, 1999).

16  Anne Jensen (trans. and comm.), *Thekla: die Apostolin: ein apokrypher Text neu entdeckt* (Freiburg im Breisgau: Herder, 1995).

17  I am grateful to Averil Cameron for this point.

## Women as overseers of house churches

The New Testament shows the apostles as peripatetic preachers, whilst local congregations frequently took the form of house churches, generally led – which is to say overseen – by the head of the household in which they met. These leaders too were not only men; indeed in the NT accounts and in Paul's greetings women predominate, and the majority of male house church leaders mentioned by Paul are named together with a woman. We hear of the establishment of a church in the house of Lydia (Acts 16.14–15, 40). Acts 12.12–17 seems to witness to such a house church led by Mary, the mother of John Mark. Paul greets or alludes to churches in the house of Chloe (1 Cor. 1.11), Nympha (Col. 4.16), and Prisca (or Priscilla) and Aquila, evangelists who had become overseers of a house church (Rom. 16.3–5, 1 Cor. 16.19, and compare also Acts 18). In Paul's list of greetings in Romans (16.1), the deacon (masculine form: *diakonos*) Phoebe is described also as *prostatis*, a term which is often translated patron or benefactor, but which in 1 Timothy in its verb form is used to characterize the tasks of the bishop, deacon or elder (1 Tim. 3.4–5; 5.17).[18] Phoebe thus seems to exercise some function of oversight.

In the earliest Christian communities fixed patterns of leadership and oversight were not yet established. This is a period in which charism – the gift of the Spirit – was of greater importance than office. It is also a period in which the missionary apostle, whether man or woman, inevitably took a leadership role in establishing the community, and in which the host of the house church, whether man or woman, was well placed to take oversight of the community once the apostle or apostles moved on. As already noted, the terms used to refer to these leaders vary

---

18   Elisabeth Schüssler Fiorenza, *In Memory of Her: A Feminist Theological Reconstruction of Christian Origins* (London: SCM Press, 1983), pp. 47–8; cf. Elizabeth A. Castelli, 'Romans', in Elisabeth Schüssler Fiorenza (ed.), *Searching the Scriptures: A Feminist Commentary* (London: SCM Press, 1995), Vol. 2, pp. 272–300, here pp. 276–9.

and often overlap; they include *episcopos* and *presbyteros*, and perhaps also *prostatis*.

## Conflicts about leadership: the Pastoral Epistles and Ignatius of Antioch

By the time the Pastoral Epistles came to be written, probably at the very end of the first century or early in the second century, a process of structural definition had begun. The Pastoral Epistles attempt to distinguish between office-holders; in particular the terminology of bishop/deacon is used in preference to the term presbyter, and there are indications of a conflict between them.

The provisions of 1 Timothy instruct that the bishop is to be a man who has had one wife,[19] who is a householder, and of good standing in society (1 Tim. 3.1–7). Deacons are also men of good character (1 Tim. 3.8–10, 12–13). Female deacons appear also to be envisioned (1 Tim. 3.11, and probably 12–13).[20] Presbyters receive only brief mention (1 Tim. 5.17–18; Tit. 1.5), and in Titus are set equivalent to bishops. A later mention of πρεσβύτας (*presbytas*), instructing them to be temperate in character and sound in faith (Tit. 2.2), is paralleled with a similar instruction to πρεσβύτιδας (*presbytidas*: feminine form); here the terms are generally taken to refer to old men and women.

Intriguingly, there are notable parallels between the requirements in 1 Timothy for women wishing to be officially recognized as widows and those for bishops: the widows are to be women with experience of leading a household and educating children, of good standing in the community (1 Tim. 5.3–16, especially 9–10). This is interesting since in the early centuries of

---

19   There was considerable discussion in the early church about whether a widower might marry a second time. See for instance, Peter Brown, *The Body and Society: Men, Women and Sexual Renunciation in Early Christianity* (London: Faber & Faber, 1989), pp. 147–52.

20   This text has been variously interpreted, with the 'women' in 1 Tim. 3.11 being understood simply as 'women', as 'deacons' wives', or as 'female deacons'.

the Christian Church the terms widow (Greek χήρα *chēra*; Latin *vidua*) and *presbytera* seem to have been parallel, so that the term 'widow' may be used alongside the Latin *praesbytera* and *anicula* or the Greek πρεσβυτέρα (*presbytera*) and πρεσβῦτις (*presbytis*).[21] The term widow as used in Early Church texts can ambiguous. It includes widows in the modern sense – women who had outlived their husbands – but could also refer to a woman who had chosen to live a celibate or ascetic life, and in some cases to withdraw from her husband.[22] Widows were particularly associated with the temple and a life of prayer, which 1 Timothy insists must be the chief task of the enrolled widows.

Ignatius of Antioch, writing in the second century, offers a similar picture of the ministry. He compares the bishop to God, the deacon to Christ and the presbyters to the apostles, which would appear to indicate the relative values he assigned to their ministries.[23] As in the Pastoral Epistles, bishops and deacons are ascribed a more central role than presbyters. Like the author of 1 Timothy, Ignatius commends widows to a life of prayer.

However, a life of prayer might include prophecy and proclamation, as demonstrated by Anna, widow and prophet (Lk. 2.36–38).

---

21 As noted above, Jean Daniélou generally translated the feminine forms *presbytis/presbytides* as 'widow(s)': Jean Daniélou, *The Ministry of Women in the Early Church* (London: Faith Press, 1961). Compare also Christine Trevett, *Montanism. Gender, Authority and the New Prophecy* (Cambridge: Cambridge University Press, 1996), p. 187. For further discussion of the relation between widows and presbyters, see Charlotte Methuen, 'Die Autorität von Frauen', pp. 20–27. Widows could also be referred to as virgins: see Charlotte Methuen, 'The "Virgin Widow": A Problematic Social Role for the Early Church?', in *Harvard Theological Review* 90 (1997), pp. 285–98.

22 For further details of this use of the term widow, see Charlotte Methuen, 'The "virgin widow"'; and Charlotte Methuen, 'Widows, bishops and the struggle for authority in the *Didascalia Apostolorum*', in *Journal of Ecclesiastical History* 46 (1995), pp. 197–213.

23 Ignatius, epistle to the Magnesians 6; Ignatius, epistle to the Trallians 3.

In a Jewish context, Philo describes widows as 'women chosen for the holy priesthood',[24] and widows were accorded high status in many early Christian communities. Tertullian's church had widows who were responsible for counselling and caring for the women of the congregation; they took a part in interpreting prophecy, and they were seated in a prominent place, together with the bishops, elders and deacons.[25] Origen includes widows in a list of the clergy, although he notes that they are appointed rather than ordained;[26] he too uses the terminology interchangeably with *presbytides*, whom with the presbyters he instructs to 'teach truly'[27] (for widows this means responsibility for the instruction of younger women)[28]. Widows may be known as

---

24 I am indebted to Angela Standhartinger for this point. Standhartinger connects Philo's description of widows to his description of communities of *therapeuts*, who were ascetic exegetes. These communities were made up predominantly of 'elderly virgins who have ... who have [preserved their holiness] out of a free conviction and their eagerness and desire for wisdom', who lived in ascetic communities in which they can dedicate themselves to the study of divine wisdom (Philo, de vita contemplative, 22; 28–30; 68); these 'elderly virgins' might, she argues, also be termed widows.

25 See, for instance, Tertullian, de pudicicitia 13.7; de virginibus velandis, 9.3; ad uxorem 1, 7.4. Cf. Jens-Uwe Krause, *Witwen und Waisen im Römischen Reich*, Vol 4: *Witwen und Waisen im frühen Christentum* (Heidelberger Althistorische Beiträge und Epigraphische Studien 19; Stuttgart: Steiner, 1995), pp. 55–6. Thurston argues that their seating indicates that they were regarded as having clerical status, and draws attention to the complexity of translating and interpreting the phrase *sacerdotium viduitatis*: 'priesthood is of the widowed'. See Bowman Thurston, *The Widows: A Women's Ministry in the Early Church* (Minneapolis, MN: Fortress Press, 1989), pp. 88, 90.

26 Origen, de oratione, 28.4; commentarius in Johannem (in Ioh. comm.), 32, 12; see Krause, *Witwen und Waisen*, Vol. 4, pp. 56–7.

27 Origen, in Ioh. comm., 32, 12.

28 Origen, homiliae in Isaiam, 6, 3. Origen reads the instructions for admitting widows (1 Tim. 5.3–8) in connection with the instruction

*presbyterae*, that is, as female presbyters or elders, women who shared in the teaching of the congregation and who exercised authority over others (usually, but not exclusively, women, as indicated by the comments by Bishop Firmilian of Caesarea about a woman presbyter)[29].

The developments witnessed to by the Pastoral Epistles and the letters of Ignatius are almost certainly connected to developing practices of liturgy and particularly to questions of who might teach, baptize, and preside at the eucharist. However, there seems also to have been a missionary motivation behind these moves to restructure the leadership of the local Christian community. Margaret Y. MacDonald suggests that 'for a group intent on winning the world, public opinion simply could not be ignored', and that possibilities for Christian women were shaped in consequence.[30] The Pastoral Epistles and the letters of Ignatius advocate a church structure – in terms both of leadership and the roles of men and women – which was intended to be familiar to the people to whom their authors wanted the gospel to be proclaimed; as such it was reluctant to put women into leadership roles which might not be respected by the pagans to whom they wished to preach. The third-century *Didascalia Apostolorum* uses this argument quite explicitly: women should not teach, because 'the pagans will mock and scoff' if they hear the teaching of the incarnation and the resurrection from a woman.[31] The comment is telling: women are excluded from the teaching ministry (except to female catechumens who live in pagan households, who are taught by female deacons) for a pragmatic, missionary reason,

---

that 'older women should teach the younger women 'what is good' (Tit. 2.3–4).

29  Cyprian, Epistle, 75.10–11 (for further discussion, see at n. 35 below).

30  Margaret Y. MacDonald, *Early Christian Women and Pagan Opinion: The Power of The Hysterical Woman* (Cambridge: Cambridge University Press, 1996), p. 178.

31  *Didaskalia apostolorum*, ch. 15; R. Hugh Connolly, *Didascalia Apostolorum*, (Oxford: Clarendon Press, 1929), p. 132.

because the society to which the congregation is ministering does not respect words spoken by a woman. Women church leaders may not take a public, representational role.[32]

## Women with oversight?

It has been argued above that in the Early Church, the term widow is often synonymous with the Latin *praesbytera* or *anicula* and the Greek πρεσβυτερα and πρεσβυτις.[33] Whilst the masculine form of these terms has generally been translated as presbyter or elder, there has been a tendency for scholars to interpret the terms *praesbytera*, πρεσβυτερα and πρεσβυτις as referring to 'elderly women', despite the clear use of these terms in inscriptions and sources to refer to ministries. Thus the Caesarean Bishop Firmilian writes to Cyprian of a female presbyter who baptized and celebrated the eucharist.[34] The new prophecy recognized

---

32  The exclusion of women from public representative roles was a characteristic of Greek and – to a lesser extent – of Roman society. Wendy Cotter argues that Roman women had authority in the household and could hold office in clubs, but were not admitted to public, civic office: 'Women's Authority Roles in Paul's Churches: Countercultural or Conventional?', in *Novum Testamentum* 36 (1994), pp. 350–72. Cf. *Women Bishops in the Church of England?*, p. 168.

33  This use can be found in ch. 26 of the (fragmentary) Latin translation of the *Didascalia*: *Didascaliae Apostolorum Canonum Ecclesiasticorum Traditionis Apostolicae Versiones Latinae*, ed. Erik Tidner, Texte und Untersuchungen 75 (Berlin: Akademie-Verlag, 1963), fifth series, Vol. 19.

34  Cyprian, Ep. 75.10–11. This woman's authority seems to have been recognized as legitimate until it was alleged that she had been possessed by an evil spirit. The problem for Firmilian is to define the status of those who had been baptized by someone possessed, and he does not seem concerned by the fact that she was a woman. For various interpretations, all of which place this female presbyter in the context of the new prophecy, see Susanna Elm, *'Virgins of God': The Making of Asceticism in Late Antiquity* (Oxford: Clarendon Press, 1994), pp 30–32; Anne Jensen, *Gottes selbstbewußte Töchter. Frauen-*

Charlotte Methuen

female presbyters.[35] Eisen concludes from her study of
inscriptional evidence that female presbyters (*presbytides,
presbyterae, sacerdotae*) existed and oversaw congregations in East
and West until at least the fourth century.[36]

Despite its restriction on what is acceptable liturgical and
teaching activity for women, and particularly for widows, the
*Didascalia* demonstrates that women (in this case deacons under
the oversight of the bishop) continued to share responsibility for
teaching and preparing women for baptism where this was
deemed necessary for reasons of modesty, and in particular in
strongly segregated societies. In the fifth-century *Testamentum
Domini* widows have oversight over female deacons and possibly
over female presbyters in much the same way as bishops have
oversight over male deacons and presbyters.[37] A widow's place in

emanzipation im frühen Christentum? (Freiburg im Breisgau: Herder,
1992), pp. 352–8. English translation: *God's Self-Confident Daughters:
Early Christianity and the Liberation of Women* (Louisville, KY:
Westminster John Knox Press, 1996); Christine Trevett, *Montanism:
Gender, Authority and the New Prophecy* (Cambridge: Cambridge
University Press, 1996), p. 171.

35 Jensen, *Gottes selbstbewußte Töchter*, pp. 268-352, esp. pp. 331–44;
Trevett, *Montanism*, pp. 185–96. The new prophecy is often called
Montanism, after the prophet Montanus, although it was probably
founded by a female prophet, Prisca.

36 Eisen, *Amtsträgerinnen*, pp. 112–37.

37 *Testamentum Domini*, I, 19: the hierarchical list of clergy given in the
*Testamentum Domini* seems to be derived from the *Traditio Apostolica*,
the so-called Church Order of Hippolytus (c. AD 215, probably in
Rome), and lists widows fifth in a hierarchy of nine orders and
functions. In the *Traditio Apostolica*, as in the *Testamentum Domini*,
widows are preceded by the bishop, presbyter, deacon and
confessors. After the widows are listed reader (*lector*), virgin, sub-
deacon and those with the gift of healing. The *Traditio Apostolica*
emphasizes that, unlike a bishop, presbyter or deacon, a widow is
not ordained but 'named'. In the *Testamentum Domini*, however,
although widows are listed after the bishop, male and female
presbyters, deacons and male and female confessors, it is explicitly

85

church was next to the bishop. She was responsible for the teaching of women, the examination of female deacons, for prayer, for anointing the sick and for anointing at baptism.[38]

There are therefore strong parallels between widows and presbyters, but there is evidence too that the office of widow was originally closely related to that of bishop.[39] We have seen the parallels between the requirements for bishops and widows in 1 Timothy. Other later widows are also referred to with terms generally used for bishops: thus we hear of a widow 'who sat in the basilica,' in the same way that a bishop might be said to sit or be seated.[40] The use of the terms *presbyteros* and *episcopos* to refer to the same person or group of people in Acts and in Titus are a reminder that in the process of establishing these offices, the two could be merged. It is thus conceivable that while in many parts of the Church women were no longer allowed to exercise authority except through giving money to finance certain ministries,[41] in others widows or female presbyters became the equivalent of female bishops, perhaps with particular responsibility for those (women) ministering to women, and that they may even have been accorded this title.

Canon 14 of the Council of Tours offers evidence for this interpretation, for it explicitly counters the idea that women must minister to women: 'a bishop who has no *episcop[i]a* may not include women amongst his entourage; for see, as man has been saved by the faith of woman, so too woman is saved by the faith

---

stated that they are ordained, and that a widow's seat in the church is beside that of the bishop.

38  *Test. Dom.* I, 40.

39  Eisen, *Amsträgerinnen*, p. 149.

40  Morris, *Against Nature* and *God*, p. 6: 'Riexem ppli annv vidva sedit basilica asvisv ravit qui obit est.'

41  For the authority of female patrons, see Elizabeth A. Clark, 'Patrons, Not Priests: Gender and Power in Late Ancient Christianity', in *Gender and History* 2 (1990), pp. 255–73.

## Charlotte Methuen

of man, as the apostle said'.[42] Women are therefore not necessary as ministers in the Church, and other clergy may be delegated to take over their responsibilities, including looking after the bishop if his wife or sister cannot take responsibility for this task.[43] However, Tours does seem to know of female clergy: Canon 20 emphasizes that married clergy should stay where their wives are, but sleep separately from them, whilst unmarried clergy must also sleep separately, and not 'the *presbiter* with his *presbiteria*, or the *diaconus* with his *diaconissa* or the *subdiaconus* with his *subdiaconissa*', on pain of excommunication and defrocking.[44] Whilst *presbiteria*, *diaconissa* and *subdiaconissa* could possibly refer to the wives of the married clergy, as the apparatus of the edition suggests,[45] the structure of the argument suggests rather that the Council of Tours is seeking to discourage clergy who are accustomed to working in male–female celibate pairs from doing so.[46] In any case it is clear that the Council of Tours is familiar

---

42  'Episcopum episcop[i]am non habentem nulla sequatur turba mulierem; *videlicet* saluatur *vir per mulierem fidelem, sicut et mulier per virum fidelem*, ut apostolus ait,' concilium Turonensi (Conc. Turon.), canon 14 (13), in CCSL 148A, p. 181 (my italics).

43  Canon 13 (12) instructs that the Bishop should be looked after by his wife or sister if she is one of the faithful (CCSL 148A, p. 180). 'Nam ubi talis custodia necessaria non est, quid necesse est, ut miseria prosequatur, unde fama consurgat? Habeant ministri ecclesiae, untique clerici, qui episcopum serviunt et eum custodire debent, licentiam extraneas mulieres de frequentia quohabitionis eiecere' (CCSL 148A, p. 181).

44  Conc. Turon., canon 20 (19), in: CCSL 148A, p. 184.

45  CCSL 148A, p. 184. The Canons of the Council of Tours explicitly use the term 'wife' (*uxor*) to refer to the wives of married clergy, including the wife of a Bishop. For the case of *episcopia*, see Eisen, *Amtsträgerinnen*, pp. 194–5.

46  The so-called *agapetai* or *virgines subintroductae* emerge as a possible problem in the second century, create problems for Cyprian and continue to appear in condemnations of councils into the fifth or sixth centuries: see Margaret Miles, 'Patriarchy as Political Theology: The Establishment of North African Christianity', in

with a parallel clerical terminology of *episcopia*, *presbiteria*, *diaconissa* and *subdiaconissa* and with a theological tradition which taught that women could be brought to salvation only by women. Perhaps the 'venerable lady, bishop Q—' in sixth-century Umbria (contemporaneous to the Council of Tours), the anonymous 'honourable lady, bishop' and the Episcopa Theodora belonged to that tradition, and were indeed female bishops: women with oversight over female officeholders or clergy in a church which had retained parallel structures of male and female clergy.

### The 'heresy' of women's leadership

Structures of leadership and oversight in the Church, including the establishment of the episcopate as the principal pattern of oversight, were developed in response to particular situations, determined at least in part by the *mores* – and consequently the needs – of the social context in which a particular church community was ministering. Some of these *mores* involved the exclusion of women from positions of public leadership, and these too were taken over by the Church.

There is no doubt that women's leadership was contested from an early date: the gospel accounts of the resurrection hint at a conflict about whether Mary Magdalen and the other women were capable of bearing witness. Tertullian condemns churches which recognize the leadership of women. However, the association between women's leadership and heresy appears to strengthen at about the time that the monarchical episcopate was becoming firmly established.

Virginia Burrus has shown that during the fourth century, theologians began to re-categorize previously 'orthodox' writings

Leroy S. Rouner (ed.), *Civil Religion and Political Theology* (Notre Dame, IN: University of Notre Dame Press, 1986), pp. 169–86, here 178–9. Cf. Hans Achelis, *Virgines Subintroductae: Ein Beitrag zu 1 Cor. VII* (Leipzig: J. C. Hinrichs, 1902); and (rather more recently) Susanna Elm, *'Virgins of God'*, who traces clergy living with ascetic women, including widows and deaconesses (p. 206).

as 'heretical' simply on the grounds that they offered evidence for women's leadership, and she points to a 'feminizing tendency' in the definition of heresy from the fourth century onwards.[47] This tendency leads into a closed circle of interpretation. Epiphanius, convinced that women should not exercise (sacramental) authority within the Church, develops an image of the 'true' or 'orthodox' Church which complies with his own views, in this case a Church without women in leadership roles or as office-holders. In support of this understanding of the 'true', 'orthodox' Church, he refers to writings which supported his view as 'orthodox', rejecting those which do not support his view as 'heretical', regardless of the fact that in their own time and place, these views might have been seen as entirely orthodox. This closed circle of interpretation exhibits itself in the transformation of Junia into Junias by Giles of Rome, and can still be observed today, as shown by the 'Mrs Bishop' reading of the *femina episcopa* inscriptions discussed above.[48]

### The challenge to today's Church: that the Gospel be heard

I have argued that it was ultimately for pragmatic reasons that the male episcopacy took the ascendancy: as a familiar leadership structure, derived from secular institutions and conforming to the social expectations of the elite, it enabled the Church to gain a firm foothold in the society to which it was reaching out to preach the gospel. However, the establishment of the (male) episcopate was not a simple process, as the canons and acts of councils and synods show. Women continued to exercise authority and oversight in the Church, even if their office was sometimes

---

47 Virginia Burrus, 'The Heretical Woman as Symbol in Alexander, Athanasius, Epiphanius and Jerome', in *Harvard Theological Review* 84 (1991), pp. 229-48. Cf. Eisen, *Amtsträgerinnen*, pp. 116–19.
48 Cf. the interpretations of the women listed after the deacons in 1 Tim. 3, who have variously been understood as a group of women, as the wives of deacons or as women deacons in their own right.

controversial.[49] Medieval examples of women with oversight persisted, as shown by the quasi-episcopal leadership and independent jurisdiction of the abbesses and prioresses of medieval monasteries and canoness orders such as Hilda's foundation at Whitby, or French Jouarre, Italian Conversano, and German Quedlinburg and Essen.[50] Patterns of ministry, and patterns of involvement of men and women in leadership and oversight, were not and have never been fixed throughout the history of the Church, but have developed and changed as the centuries passed. Many of the decisions of the Early Church about its leadership structures were mission-driven, and some of those excluding women from ministry were intended to prevent the institution of the Church from becoming a stumbling-block or an embarrassment to those to whom the folly of the gospel was to be preached.

Perhaps this is a principle that could guide us too as we debate the future patterns of ministry in our church. In the missionary situation in which our churches increasingly find themselves in the Western world, as Margaret Miles has suggested, 'we are challenged, as were the earliest Christian communities, to service based on talent, regardless of gender'.[51] The challenge to us is to determine, as the early Christians did, how best we may bring the gospel to those who are in most need of it. We live in a society in which women's voices are increasingly heard and respected, in which women work alongside men in secular employment and may take leadership as required. There are scriptural precedents for women who spread the faith as apostles and evangelists, or

---

49  Lyman, 'Women Bishops in Antiquity', p. 45.

50  See, for instance, Morris, *Against Nature and God*. For Essen, see Ute Küppers-Braun, *Macht im Frauenhand: 1000 Jahre Herrschaft adeliger Frauen in Essen* (Essen: Klartext, 2002). The abbesses of Quedlinberg and Essen held their authority directly from the pope and the emperor with no intervening episcopal jurisdiction; in Essen the abbess retained this status until secularization under Napoleon in 1802.

51  Miles, 'Patriarchy as Political Theology', p. 184.

who had oversight over house churches and other Christian communities. The tradition of the Church suggests that the exclusion of women from those offices came about for reasons of mission, for fear that the pagans would 'mock and scoff' to hear women teach. Today, this is no longer the context in which we preach the gospel. Indeed, in our context one might argue that the situation is reversed, and that the refusal to reverse this decision is rather a reason for people to 'mock and scoff' at preachers of the gospel, seeing the Church as 'anachronistic and odd'.[52]

And let us not forget Chrysostom: 'For an honour we have, in that there are such women amongst us.' The Church today is enriched and honoured by the gifts of many of its women priests. Surely it can only be an impoverishment if such women cannot be called to serve the Church as bishops? Let us, with Chrysostom, affirm that we are indeed honoured that there are such women amongst us, and let us rejoice that women are ready to partake of the labours of the Church for the gospel's sake, and to 'perform all ministries'.

---

52 As suggested by Carrie Pemberton, 'We Wish You Were Here: Some Views from the Pews', in *The Call for Women Bishops*, pp. 175–83, here p. 176.

# 8

## Anglo-Catholics and the Myths of Episcopacy

### MARK D. CHAPMAN

### Anglo-Catholics and bishops

Anglo-Catholicism has always had a fixation with bishops: a great deal has been invested in the office and function of the successors to the apostles, so much so that bishops have become central to Anglo–Catholic self-definition. This was true from the very beginning of the movement. As the Swedish archbishop and church historian, Yngve Brilioth wrote (with some justification): 'One must ask whether at any time in the history of the church the office of bishop has been so immediately exalted to the clouds as in these early tracts.'[1] The reason was straightforward. Bishops provided something of a substitute for the perceived collapse of traditional patterns of authority in the British state and English church of the 1820s and '30s. Bishops, or more precisely a particular understanding of the theory of episcopacy rooted in a somewhat supernatural understanding of 'apostolical succession' (or episcopal plumbing), provided the basis for Tractarian claims about the independence of an ecclesiastical authority distinct from that of the state.

This was clear from as early as Newman's *Thoughts on the Ministerial Commission*, the first of the *Tracts for the Times*, which was published on 9 September 1833.[2] He addressed the simple question: if the ministerial commission no longer came from the government, then where did it come from?

---

1 Yngve Brilioth, *The Anglican Revival: Studies in the Oxford Movement* (London: Longmans, 1933), p. 192.
2 *Thoughts on the Ministerial Commission, Respectfully Addressed to the Clergy* (London: Rivington, 1833).

> Should the government and country so far forget their God
> as to cast off the church, to deprive it of its temporal
> honours and substance, *on what* will you rest the claim of
> respect and attention which you make upon your flocks?

For Newman, the answer was clear: the real ground upon 'which
our authority is built [is] OUR APOSTOLICAL DESCENT'. And he goes
on to provide a description of what he meant by this:

> We have been born, not of blood, nor of the will of the
> flesh, nor of the will of man, but of God. The Lord JESUS
> CHRIST gave His Spirit to His Apostles; they in turn laid
> their hands on those who would succeed them; and these
> again on others and these again on others; and so the
> sacred gift has been handed down to our present Bishops,
> who have appointed us as their assistants, and in some
> sense representatives ... We must necessarily consider *none*
> to be ordained who have not been thus ordained. ... Exalt
> our Holy Fathers the Bishops, as the Representatives of the
> Apostles, and the Angels of the Churches; and magnify
> your office, as being ordained by them to take part in their
> ministry.

While some of the 'Angels of the Churches' of the 1830s were no
doubt more than a little surprised at this elevation of their status, it is
an idea that stuck, proving deeply influential on succeeding
generations for whom it became a badge or marker of identity. This
emphasis on bishops was coupled with a historical myth: unlike the
dissenters and the Protestant churches of Europe, the Church of
England stood in continuity with the Early Church, with the
obvious implication that the Reformation had little effect other than
to purify the Church of the worst abuses of the Roman system.[3] The

---

3    Diarmaid MacCulloch, 'The Myth of the English Reformation', in
     *Journal of British Studies* 30 (1991), pp. 1–19.

Prayer Book Ordinal provided good ammunition with its assumption that it is 'evident unto all men diligently reading holy Scripture and ancient authors, that from the apostles' time, there have been orders of ministry in Christ's Church; bishops, priests and deacons'. For many Anglo-Catholics it was much easier to claim continuity with the pre-Reformation heritage in the doctrine of ministry than in virtually anything else. In the emphatic (if misleading) words of a fairly recent official Church of England report on *Episcopal Ministry*:

> There was no intention in the Henrician, Edwardine or Elizabethan legislation to make any fundamental change in the understanding of the nature of episcopal ministry, or to allow any interruption in the succession, for the English Reformers believed they saw a clear Scriptural warrant for episcopal ministry.[4]

While there is an element of truth in this statement in that the Church of England retained something that was lost in many other reformed churches, it nevertheless tends to suggest that what is important about episcopacy is the simple fact of continuity with the past.

The fact that episcopacy was practised quite differently after the Reformation, and its theological underpinning quite transformed, is frequently left unexplored. With few exceptions, most writers sympathetic to bishops before the English Civil War period based their arguments on decency and good order rather than on apostolic succession.[5] Very few – and that even included such figures as William Laud – were willing to see bishops as necessary for the constitution of the Church. On the whole they accepted the ministry and sacraments of the continental Protestant churches as expressions

---

4    *Episcopal Ministry: The Report of the Archbishops' Commission on the Episcopate 1990* (London: Church House Publishing, 1990), p. 79.
5    On this, see my 'The Politics of Episcopacy', in *Bishops, Saints and Politics: Anglican Studies* (London: T&T Clark, 2007), pp. 9–32.

of the true Church relative to their particular contexts. 'Sacramental assurance', a term used in both the Rochester and Guildford reports,[6] was not guaranteed by episcopal succession, but by the intention expressed in Article VII of the Augsburg Confession, which was loosely translated as Article XIX of the Thirty-nine Articles: 'The visible Church of Christ is a congregation of faithful men, in which the pure Word of God is preached, and the Sacraments duly ministered.' Indeed, nowhere in the Thirty-nine Articles is there any account given about the nature and importance of bishops and their necessity for the visible Church. By the 1830s, however, by the time of Tract 4, John Keble could assert that the Church of England was 'the only church in this realm which has a right to be quite sure that she has the Lord's Body to give to his people'.[7] The validity of orders, and consequently the doctrine of sacramental assurance, had become central to Tractarian theology, even though they were foreign to much earlier theology.

## Bishops against Protestants

Sometimes the elevation of the episcopate above virtually everything else became almost pathological. One of the best historical examples is the dispute over the establishment of a joint English and Prussian bishopric in Jerusalem in 1841.[8] The idea, which was put forward by the Prussian king through his theologically literate minister, Baron Christian von Bunsen, was to create a shared bishop for both

---

6    *Women in the Episcopate: the Guildford Group Report* (London: Church House Publishing, 2006), Appendix 2, p. 43; *Women Bishops in the Church of England* (London: Church House Publishing, 2005), pp. 144–5.

7    *Adherence to the Apostolical Succession the Safest Course* (London: Rivington, 1833), p. 4.

8    On the Jerusalem bishopric see Martin Lückhoff, *Anglikaner und Protestanten im Heiligen Land. Das gemeinsame Bistum Jerusalem (1841– 1886)* (Wiesbaden: Harrassowitz, 1998), esp. ch. 6. There is little evidence that the Prussians sought to gain apostolic succession from the Church of England.

churches. The obvious problem was that one of the churches involved claimed bishops in the apostolic succession, and the other understood bishops quite differently. Initially, opinion among the Anglo-Catholics was divided. Dr Pusey, by that stage the movement's leader, was enthusiastic. He wrote to Howley, Archbishop of Canterbury, about the merits of the scheme. The Lutherans would 'be absorbed into our Church to which they had united themselves, and gradually imbibe her spirit and be Catholicized. I trusted to the Catholicity of our Church to win those who were brought within the sphere of her influence.'[9] Others, including Newman, were less enthusiastic: Lutheranism and Calvinism had been condemned as heresies by both the Eastern Orthodox and Roman Catholic churches, which meant a shared episcopate would be quite impossible and would compromise the catholic nature of the Church of England. Others still, including Frederick Oakeley of Margaret Street Chapel, London, were anxious about the very idea of national churches, which they regarded as uncatholic:

> The Catholic Church is not, as I believe, a collection of separate bodies forming an aggregate, of circles as in a river, touching one another, and forming a collection of circles, but one circle which has so entirely absorbed all others into itself that no trace of their independence remains. Now what the King of Prussia appears and is said to wish is to consolidate a Protestant National Church; and looking upon the Church of England as a sister Protestant body, with the advantage of a better government, he comes to us to borrow our form of the government with the view of combining discordant elements, and securing external peace and union among his subjects. All this, I can quite conceive, in a good average Sovereign, and an amiable but

---

9    In H. P. Liddon, *The Life of Edward Bouverie Pusey* (London: Longmans, 1894), 4 Vols, Vol. 2, p. 250.

not very high-minded and deep-thinking and far-seeing man.

Oakeley's main charge was that 'Erastianism is, at all events, so very like a form of Antichrist, and foreign Protestantism'.[10] To give episcopacy to the Prussians, when they were not prepared to amend their ways and give up their Protestant inheritance, would compromise the very nature of the Church itself.

After the convert Jewish rabbi, Michael Solomon Alexander was consecrated in November 1841, there were a number of responses: William Palmer of Magdalen College, Oxford, wrote to the Archbishop complaining of 'the admission of persons of the Lutheran persuasion to the communion of the new Bishop', and against 'the erection of a bishopric within the Dioceses of the Oriental Churches'.[11] Similarly, Pusey began to attack the scheme with its implied recognition of Calvinism and Lutheranism, which might infect the English church with the horrors of rationalism. As the example of seventeenth-century Scotland proved, he felt, it was no good offering people the episcopate until they were ready for it. He wrote to the Archbishop:

There is at present even in the sounder part of the Luthero-Calvinist body, not a vestige, among its writers, of the first condition of a sound restoration, – humility; ... the few who look for Episcopacy seem to desire it, in order to organize their imperfections, not to correct them; the most religious of their theological organs declare against the Catholic view of it; they distinctly tell us that it is looked upon not as anything spiritual, but as an outward mechanism; they tell us that the people desire it not; they refute the notion (and with good ground) that any changes recently proposed among themselves are any symptoms of

---

10  Oakeley to Pusey, 16 November 1841, in Liddon, *Pusey*, Vol. 2, pp. 254–5.
11  Palmer to Howley, in Liddon, *Pusey*, Vol. 2, p. 256.

such longing; there has been the wish to extend Presbyterian ordination, where now there is none; no desire of Episcopal. It is for your Grace and your Grace's brethren to consider how, in such a state of mind, you could, without profanation, entrust a gift of the Holy Spirit, which is undesired, set at nought, repudiated, by those who are to receive it.

Consequently Pusey expressed serious doubts about the possibility of merging with what he regarded as the inadequate church of Protestant Prussia:

> Your Grace expresses a hope that this Bishopric 'may lead the way to an essential unity of discipline as well as doctrine between our own Church and the less perfectly constituted of the Protestant Churches of Europe, i.e. that they will be one Church, through the Absorption of the Lutherans into our Church, and the reception, on their part, of all those things for lack of which they are at present imperfect'. Their view is wholly different; they look to this same event, only as an aggrandizement of their own body, ... they look to it as an occasion for developing the German Evangelical Church, according to '*the Confession*, and *with the use of the liturgy*, of that Church'.[12]

The effect of the Anglo-Prussian bishopric would be to promote the corruptions of German Protestantism. Similarly, William Gladstone felt that the 'mingled Church' was at the same time an 'experimental Church' which would compromise the very principles of the Church of England, even allowing such uncatholic practices as sitting while singing hymns. It would be led by pastors 'consenting to receive Episcopal Ordination, but not, as [they?]

---

12  Liddon, *Pusey*, Vol. 2, pp. 258–9.

themselves contend, valuing it.'[13] Episcopacy was not something to be shared without serious repercussions.

Within a few years, when the time came to appoint the Lutheran pastor Samuel Gobat as second occupant of the bishopric in 1846 after Alexander's sudden death, Pusey was firm in his opposition. Indeed, he was almost obsessive in his hostility about donating episcopacy to a heretical church:

> What a misery it would be if the ultimate object of the Prussian Government were attained, and they were to receive Episcopacy from us, and we were to become the authors of an heretical Succession. I should think it would split the English Church at once; it would put one, if one lived to see it, in a most distressing position. To be alive to heresy is a mark of full soundness of faith. To give Episcopacy to Prussia now, or even to prepare for it, is like arraying a corpse, or whitening a sepulchre. Surely, while they are struggling for the very elements of the faith, recovering what they can, indifferent about some doctrines, hostile to others, it would be very miserable to mix ourselves up with them or commit to them so sacred a deposit.[14]

Even more extraordinary in its vehemence is Pusey's letter to Benjamin Harrison, written a few days later. Giving episcopacy to the heretical church of Prussia, he claimed, amounted to

> a recognition of Evangelicalism on our part, not of the necessity, or even expediency, of Episcopacy on theirs. We commit ourselves to Lutheranism; the King of Prussia alone commits himself to Episcopacy. The Jerusalem Bishopric is a sort of experiment on the part of the King of Prussia, how far his subjects can be familiarized to

---

13  Liddon, *Pusey*, Vol. 2, p. 257.
14  Pusey to Gladstone, 9 April 1846, in Liddon, *Pusey*, Vol. 3, p. 71.

Episcopacy, as a better sort of government than their own, without any idea of any spiritual gift through it. But were this to succeed, things would be far worse. A jealous heedfulness against inter-mingling with heretics has, you know, always been a mark of the Church. To be the parent of an heretical Succession would be very miserable. Yet I suppose there would scarcely be an individual among the German Protestants who holds the true doctrine of the Sacraments, or the Nicene Creed as it was held by the Fathers at Nicaea. And this is one thing which people feel so keenly. Whereas the English Church has, since the separation, always been rising upwards towards the early Church, this is mingling her with those whom the early Church would have counted heretical. ... I did hope that the sudden death of Bishop Alexander might be of God's Providence, to put an end to the Jerusalem Bishopric. ... I cannot say what an exceeding blessing a suspension of the Jerusalem Bishopric would be. I hope to pray earnestly for it. It would make one breathe again. ... I feel as [if] I could bless God more fervently for the suspension of the Jerusalem bishopric than for the life of a dying child: by how much the church must be dearer to one than one's own life or one's child.[15]

As Peter Nockles remarks, the Jerusalem bishopric, not surprisingly in the light of such passion, 'marked an outpouring of unqualified Tractarian hostility towards the continental reformed churches hitherto unparalleled in the Church of England'.[16] Bishops were a sign that the Church of England was not the same kind of church as the Prussian church – and by extension any other

---

15  Pusey to Harrison, 13 April 1846, in Liddon, *Pusey*, Vol. 3, p. 75.
16  Peter Nockles, *The Oxford Movement in Context* (Cambridge: Cambridge University Press, 1994), p. 158. For an assessment of the Tractarian fixation on what Paul Avis calls the 'apostolic paradigm', see esp. pp. 156–64.

Protestant church. To court union was to meddle with the heresy of
the Reformation, to which, it seems, the Church of England had
never really succumbed.

What this episode reveals is that the Puseyite passion for
episcopacy was tied up with an understanding of bishops as
guardians not simply of faith, but of a very particular kind of faith,
one that distanced the Church of England from the Reformation and
the various forms of doctrine and church polity that emerged from
it. Episcopacy, on their model, was not simply located in the person
and authority of the institution as a form of church order, but was
part of a broader understanding of the Church of England based on
the myth of continuity with the Early Church, which downplayed
the English Reformation and consequently the reformed heritage of
the English church. The almost mystical elevation of bishops into an
angelic host became one of the means of redefining the Church of
England, and at the same time it helped distance the Church from
the state. The Tractarian argument was straightforward: the Church
of England had been betrayed by an apostate government, and
consequently had to assert its own independence. As Newman
wrote: 'The King ... has literally betrayed us. ... Our first duty is the
defence of the Church. We have stood by Monarchy and Authority
till they have refused to stand by themselves.'[17]

## The usefulness of bishops

The Tractarian understanding of bishops was far removed from the
shape and understanding of episcopacy which dominated thinking
in the years following the break with Rome. The most important
argument in favour of bishops in the Elizabethan period was not
that bishops were commanded in scripture, and that other forms of
ministry were inadequate, but rather, that bishops provided the most
useful means for ensuring decency and good order in the Church.[18]

17  Newman to R. F. Wilson, 8 September 1833 in *The Letters and
    Diaries of John Henry Newman* (Oxford: Clarendon Press, 1980),
    Vol. 4, p. 44.
18  Chapman, 'The Politics of Episcopacy', pp. 13–22.

For instance, Archbishop Whitgift defends bishops against the presbyterian demand for the equality of ministers in terms of their function in maintaining discipline:

> The Archbishop doth exercise his jurisdiction under the prince and by the prince's authority. For, the prince having the supreme government of the realm, in all causes and over all persons, as she doth exercise the one by the lord chancellor, so doth she the other by the archbishops.[19]

Bishops may have had a divine authority, but it was not primarily understood in terms of apostolic succession; instead it was a kind of delegated authority from the divinely anointed sovereign. Obedience to the bishop was but one aspect of obedience to the God-given laws of the English state. The Tractarian revival of the doctrine of apostolic succession as the (supernatural) basis for the authority of the Church more or less replaced the alternative models of sovereignty – the unbridled authority of the king in parliament – which had underpinned the traditional Anglican settlement and determined the practice of episcopacy. As Ingolf Dalferth, an exasperated Lutheran dialogue partner, put it in discussions about the Meissen agreement: 'To put it bluntly, one could say that the driving forces in the development of the Anglican theology of episcopacy were not primarily or exclusively theological, but always also (church) political considerations.'[20]

Discussions about episcopacy reveal much about a whole range of church political issues that has little to do with the matter of bishops

---

19  *The Works of John Whitgift* (Parker Society, Cambridge: Cambridge University Press, 1851), 3 Vols, Vol. 2, p. 248.

20  See esp. Ingolf Dalferth, 'Ministry and the Office of Bishop according to Meissen and Porvoo', in *Visible Unity and the Ministry of Oversight*, pp. 9–48, here p. 25; Geoffrey Wainwright, 'Is Episcopal Succession a Matter of Dogma for Anglicans?' in Colin Podmore (ed.), *Community–Unity–Communion* (London: Church House Publishing, 1997), pp. 164–79. *The Meissen Agreement Texts* §16, p. 18.

*per se*. There is a whole range of issues that the various discussions about bishops conceal. In most accounts there is very little mentioned about the actual practice of episcopacy. So much energy is expended on showing how modern bishops are in some sort of continuity with bishops in the Early Church and fulfil the same sort of function (as, for instance, signs of unity of time and space and of apostolicity), that there is often remarkably little discussion about how episcopacy works in the modern Church.[21] Anti-Protestantism and Tractarian historiography have frequently served to overplay the role of some atypical theologians (like Jeremy Taylor) who defended bishops at the expense of those who regarded them simply as the most useful tools for the exercise of oversight. Even William Laud saw little difference between the Lutheran superintendent and the English bishop,[22] despite the absence of a Lutheran doctrine of apostolic succession. The argument was simple: oversight was necessary, and there were various ways of exercising it. Departing from the pre-Reformation historical model was not to be recommended, but it could be done in certain cases, and it did not mean that those who had done it were necessarily unchurched. Even after the Act of Uniformity in 1662 the 'validity' of foreign churches, at least within their own territories, was seldom questioned. In the eighteenth century, William Wake (1657–1737), Archbishop of Canterbury, could write to Père Le Courayer, who had been concerned that Archbishop Grindal had granted a licence to a presbyterian minister: 'I should be unwilling to affirm that where the ministry is not episcopal, there is no church, nor any true

21 See the classic works: Kenneth Kirk (ed.), *The Apostolic Ministry: Essays on the History and Doctrine of Episcopacy* (London: Hodder & Stoughton, 1946); Claude Jenkins and K. D. Mackenzie (eds), *Episcopacy Ancient and Modern* (London: SPCK, 1930). The most comprehensive account of the practice of Episcopacy was Glyn Simon, *Bishops: What They Are and What They Do* (London: Faith Press, 1961).

22 *The Works of William Laud* (Library of Anglo-Catholic Theology, Oxford: Parker, 1849), Vol. 3, p. 386.

administration of the sacraments.'[23] Tractarians departed from this Anglican norm.

## Some lessons for the present

In what remains of this chapter, I will try to draw out some possible lessons from these excursions into the history of the Church for the matter under discussion, that is, the effect on church order of the proposed legislation on women bishops. The first point concerns the idea that there is such a thing as 'the Catholic doctrine of episcopacy'. As I have suggested, apostolic succession (with its attendant theories of sacramental validity) is simply one understanding, and became dominant again in the nineteenth century primarily for political reasons, as a way of asserting the un-Protestant nature of the Church of England, as well its independence from an apostate state. Overemphasis on this understanding, however, means that scant regard is paid to other expressions of episcopacy, including more 'corporate' understandings of episco-pacy which have developed in recent years. Yet a more thoroughgoing and less 'theological' understanding of bishops might have added much to the Guildford report. In some instances, many people are involved in the range of functions called episcopacy, only one of whom will be called a bishop. Some of those involved in *episcope* may not even be ordained at all: a bishop, after all, receives some form of oversight from the synods of the Church of England and the Archbishops' Council, which are far more reminiscent of presbyterian order than (so-called) catholic order, even though there is a lack of coherence and clarity about precisely how these are meant to function. In much the same way, it should be said, Elizabeth I exercised oversight over her church, often by ensuring that there were no bishops appointed so that her advisers could run the Church in their place.

The corporate and sometimes non-ordained dimension of *episcope* has often usurped the personal, and seems far more in tune with the

---

23  Cited in Norman Sykes, *William Wake* (Cambridge: Cambridge University Press, 1957), Vol. 2, p. 14.

democratic structures of modern forms of political and ecclesiastical authority. This means that a discussion of bishops apart from their wider context in ecclesiastical and political structures can easily detract from the changing nature of ecclesial authority and forms of oversight. Bishops alone (as Anglo-Catholics have frequently used to their advantage) often have very little authority. Whatever the theory, oversight proves remarkably difficult in a church which retains freehold and where the exercise of power proves virtually impossible. As Principal Fairbairn of Mansfield College, Oxford, remarked many years ago: the clergy who plead most 'for an apostolic episcopate as the condition for catholic unity, defer least to the episcopal voice'.[24] Or as Frank Weston, the great Bishop of Zanzibar, put it during the heady days of Anglo-Catholic triumphalism in the 1920s: 'I am not asking for obedience to a bishop. I ask for obedience to the bishops in so far as they themselves obey the Catholic Church.'[25] Authority has to be won through dialogue and conversation and in relation to the rest of the church polity (including synods) – and that goes equally for male and female bishops. The theory of bishops with authority as guardians of faith is all well and good, but the practice is usually quite different.

If this far vaguer understanding of episcopacy has a direct implication for the proposals set out in the Bishop of Guildford's report, it is this: the various aspects of episcopal authority are in practice already exercised by different people. Episcopacy is consequently a corporate rather than a personal matter; to suggest that there is an inseparable link between sacramental and jurisdictional authority is unproven.[26] As the experience of the Act of Synod has shown (albeit fairly incoherently) canonical obedience in all things lawful implies nothing about whether a congregation

---

24  A. M. Fairbairn, *Catholicism: Roman and Anglican* (London: Hodder & Stoughton, 1899), p. xxi.
25  Cited in H. A. Wilson, *Received with Thanks* (Oxford: Mowbray, 1940), p. 118.
26  See below, Appendix: Document 3.

accepts a bishop's sacramental authority. If (as at present) a bishop who ordains a woman is no longer considered to have sacramental authority in a particular parish, then it makes little difference in practice whether that bishop is a woman. It may be wishful thinking to suppose that people who think that women cannot be ordained will take an oath of canonical obedience to a woman, but there is little in the history of the Church of England that suggests that this is inconsistent or incoherent, and it is certainly less incoherent than the somewhat bizarre ideas behind the Act of Synod. After all, jurisdictional authority, as the Report admits, is sometimes undertaken by laypeople.[27]

## Episcopacy as practised

My second point is related to the first: it is worth bearing in mind that the practice of episcopacy is very different from its theory and theology. As my discussion of the Jerusalem bishopric suggested, theology so often masks what is going on at other levels. There is frequently much talk about communion between the local and the universal and the interaction between the two (as the rather pointless chapter in *Episcopal Ministry* about the Trinity is supposed to demonstrate),[28] but there is very little anywhere about the importance of the local and the experience on the ground: bishops are considered representatives of the catholic Church, but at the same time the experience of oversight is always expressed in the local. As Gregory Baum put it in relation to Vatican II: 'the entire gift of God is experienced in the local'.[29] Bishops are not some magical entities who persist apart from the local (a danger inherent in the Tractarian view) but they always relate to localities. They help bind them together with one another, try to stop them squabbling

---

27  See Guildford Report, Appendix 6.
28  *Episcopal Ministry*, ch. 2.
29  Commentary to Edward H. Peters (ed.), *De Ecclesia: The Constitution on the Church* (London: Darton, Longman and Todd, 1964), p. 21. See *Lumen Gentium*, in Austin Flannery (ed.), *Vatican Council II* (Dublin: Dominican Publications, 1975), p. 350.

too much, but ultimately they are nothing without the people of God. Their duty (and the duty of the synod which shares oversight with them) is to ensure that the gospel is preached and the sacraments duly administered on the ground, and in this they will frequently exercise their *episcope* with others.

If one looks at local churches, the forms and experience of oversight are often complex and involve the Church in a whole network of authority structures, some formal and some informal, but many assuming some sort of role of oversight. There is, for instance, an office called a team rector in the Church of England, whose role is episcopal in the sense that he or she is supposed to oversee ministry in the team. At the same time, some other churches prefer to receive oversight from party networks with their own structures, which may not be official but which effectively decide on the acceptability of certain practices and thus exercise oversight. I would suggest that before transferring oversight to a distant regional bishop, it would be worth investigating what sorts of oversight already exist and to analyse them in detail; and it would not be out of place to work out the legal and practical implications of a Forward in Faith team vicar working in the team of a female rector who is legally the incumbent of the whole benefice, but who may not be allowed to exercise a sacramental ministry in that parish. Again the stress on the personal episcopate prevents a detailed study of the breadth of oversight as it has developed in the Church of England.

## Congregations

Finally, it seems to me to be important to re-emphasize the point that the mission and ministry of the local church is the primary source of catholicity. People do not attend a universal church, but a local church which is part of a wider group of churches. It is consequently the local church that needs to be investigated in as much detail and depth as possible, not simply in terms of the functioning of episcopacy, as I suggested above, but in all its complex networks. Theological reports are all well and good but they lack much by way of an empirical basis to ascertain what precisely is going on. Too much emphasis on legal mechanics and theology at the episcopal level means that the local churches are often forgotten in theological language or the legalism of the legislative framework. This absence of a serious analysis of the local is particularly obvious in both the Rochester and Guildford Reports: surely more should have been said about why local congregations voted for resolutions A and B and opted for extended oversight.[30]

The Church of England could easily have commissioned a study of congregations, which might have been far cheaper and more useful than a theological report: as the great German theologian, Friedrich Schleiermacher well understood, statistics are sometimes just as important as theology. Numbers of resolution A, B and 'C'[31] churches are given at the back of the Guildford Report, but we know nothing at all of how big these churches are, nor what the majorities were, nor whether people came or left in response. A proper study of congregations seems imperative so that one does not rely on hearsay or on propaganda, and we do not create anomalies for the sake of a few hundred disaffected people and clergy. It may be that many of the 315 churches which have currently decided that their diocesan bishop is not welcome to exercise sacramental ministry have congregations under 50, or under 20. If that is the case it makes a difference, and probably far more difference than a study of theology. Similarly, one might ask, how many pay their parish quota in full? Tiny congregations might feel their way of ecclesiastical life is threatened – but if they are about to die anyway then might it not be better to help them (charitably) on their way to a better place? And might this perhaps be the best use of the precious resources for mission? Figures for recruits and growth are imperative

---

30 There has been remarkably little analysis of the impact of the ordination of women legislation on congregations. The Rochester report limits the discussion to a single paragraph (§4.3.1, p. 129) alluding to the important study by Ian Jones, *Women and the Priesthood in the Church of England Ten Years On* (London: Church House Publishing, 2004).

31 The term 'Resolution C' is a shorthand term used for those churches which have petitioned for extended episcopal oversight.

before more time and energy and money are spent on blowing in vain at the dying embers.

## Conclusion

By way of a brief conclusion, I simply want to suggest that the study of history might help us see the complexity of the issues, and alert us to the fact that all may not be quite as it seems. Words like 'catholic' and 'apostolic' are ambiguous and unclear, and frequently function to stifle debate and to narrow the breadth of the churches. And similarly, theological idealizations (like 'the catholic idea of episcopacy') are fictions which mask an extraordinary diversity of practices both in the past and the present. Consequently, instead of theology, I would suggest some serious sociological research is undertaken before we go any further. Firstly, we need some information about the exercise and complexity of contemporary forms of oversight and how it is expressed in all forms of ministry, lay and ordained. And secondly, and more importantly, it is crucial that we study the congregations of the Church of England, particularly those who have strong feelings on the matter under consideration. We simply do not know enough, and many are keen that the situation of ignorance should remain. But with statistics and analysis of the situation on the ground, it would be possible to make an informed judgement about whether it is time for TEA (Transferred Episcopal Arrangements), or a single clause measure. After all, the kettle has been coming to boil for a long time, and it might be better for us to wait just that little bit longer.

# 9

## *Women Bishops:*
## *A Response to Cardinal Kasper*

TOM WRIGHT AND DAVID STANCLIFFE

We greatly valued the chance to hear Cardinal Walter Kasper at the Church of England's House of Bishops meeting in June 2006, and were enormously grateful that he made the time to accept the Archbishop of Canterbury's invitation to come and address the meeting, to which a number of senior women in the Church of England had also been invited. Cardinal Kasper wrote and delivered a paper especially for the occasion, and was ready to engage in discussion with us. He came in a spirit of intellectual and theological rigour and engaged with us robustly and frankly, speaking with the clarity that goes with deep friendship. Cardinal Kasper embodies in himself and in his work the openness and warm spirit of much current ecumenical dialogue, and as we thank God for him, we offer these reflections in the same spirit of frankness, friendship and, we hope, rigour.

### To see ourselves as others see us: Rome's view of Canterbury

The fact that the Cardinal came in person at short notice speaks volumes for the depth of Rome's commitment to our shared ecumenical endeavours. As the *Tablet* leader put it:

> the fact that he agreed to address a crucial meeting of the Church of England bishops shows how close he sees the relationship and how close it is seen by the Archbishop of Canterbury ... Thus far has ecumenism travelled.[1]

---

1    *The Tablet*, 12 June 2006.

However, we were sorry that these implicit volumes did not translate in this address into spoken commitment to the Cardinal's own project, advanced elsewhere, of 'receptive ecumenism' – the project whereby Rome asks, 'what do other churches possess which we in Rome do not possess and which we therefore need to receive?' That question, and the humility of the implied stance it presupposes, is full of hopeful possibilities; some in Rome itself would see precisely developments in the ministry and episcopacy as cases in point of developments elsewhere which Rome might want to adopt. But neither the theoretical point nor that particular application appeared in the Cardinal's address.

In relation to this, we would have liked to press him further on the question of the development of doctrine, recalling the words of *Dei Verbum* II.8

> There is a growth in the understanding of the realities and the words which have been handed down [from the apostles]. This happens through the contemplation and study made by believers, who treasure these things in their hearts (cf. Lk. 2.19, 51), through the intimate understanding of spiritual things they experience, and through the preaching of those who have received through episcopal succession the sure gift of truth. For as the centuries succeed one another, the Church constantly moves forward toward the fullness of divine truth until the words of God reach their complete fulfilment in her.

What, we might ask, are the criteria by which some developments (some growths in understanding, as it were) are seen as legitimate, and others not so? For instance, the adoption of compulsory celibacy – a distinctively monastic discipline – for all ordained priests, or the Marian Dogmas of 1854 and 1952 are all viewed as acceptable developments. Others, however, including the ordination of women to the presbyterate and episcopate, Cardinal

Kasper declares the Catholic Church to be convinced that it has no right to revise its current position.

Second, we note a fundamental difference in the way in which we address theological questions. Cardinal Kasper's paper begins by quoting the correspondence between the popes and successive archbishops of Canterbury, the detailed response to the Rochester Report, and draws our attention to the various papal pronouncements on this matter before he moves to consider the biblical and patristic material. He is, understandably, concerned to defend the tradition of the Church rather than to explore what the possibilities for development might be, let alone whether the Church's traditional position of how the *imago Christi* is represented might be considered defective. So the themes he develops around the unanimity of the Early Church (quoting Acts 1.14, 2.46, 4.24 *et al*) and the nature of *koinonia* (communion) presume a more monolithic picture of the Church and of the ministry of the bishop in the service of that unity than our reading both of the events of Pentecost and of, for example, Paul's letters to the Corinthians might warrant. Unity in the life of the Early Church was marked by a great diversity of expression, and the events of Pentecost witness to a unity in the Spirit that was far from unanimous in expression. It was precisely because of this considerable diversity that writers such as Cyprian, whom the Cardinal quotes extensively, developed a theology which would secure not unity in diversity so much as uniformity.

We note that the Cardinal labels types of ecclesiology in quite precise 'catholic' and 'Protestant' categories. He is of course well aware that the Anglican Church claims to be both catholic and reformed in a way that goes beyond the sterility of at least some post-sixteenth-century debate in those terms. But the final sections of his paper continue to present a greater polarization between his type of 'catholic' theology and that of 'the Protestant churches of the sixteenth century' in a way which appear to leave no room for that type of catholic ecclesiology which the Anglican Communion has lived and developed over the last four centuries.

The Cardinal is likewise aware that *Apostolicae Curae*, Pope Leo XIII's encyclical of 1896 which pronounces Anglican orders to be 'absolutely null and utterly void', has not been rescinded in the 110 years since its promulgation. Nor has any reply been received to the response of the Archbishops of Canterbury and York of 1897, *Saepius Officio*, and this despite Vatican II's far less absolute statement that certain churches had not preserved the *'full and integral* mystery of the Eucharist'. But he hints that the road has been open to ways by which some recognition of Anglican orders might have been forthcoming – and said that to consecrate women as bishops would represent a substantial block to that option. In practice there is a 'special place' in the heart of Rome for the Anglican tradition, and for the person of the Archbishop of Canterbury, which the official formularies do not recognize.

This introduces a difficulty for us: which of these signals is genuine? There is no recognition of Anglican orders, no possibility of intercommunion, except when Anglicans are deprived of the sacraments of their own church, and little recognition of the difficulties that continue to be experienced by the children of a mixed Anglican–Roman marriage. At the same time, Rome, being concerned for the sake of the unity that God wills, is anxious to advise us on what we may and may not do with our orders, which are not regarded as valid anyway. We note that *Dominus Iesus* (2000), continued to regard Anglican churches as separated quasi-ecclesial communities. Rome regards the Eastern Orthodox as a 'church' on the grounds, in that document, that they 'objectively intend reunion' with Rome. Their *intention* is the ground of Rome's recognition – not their historic episcopate – but that same intention is to be found in the dialogue statements of Anglicans, Lutherans and Methodists. And *Ut Unum Sint* (1995) continues to regard unity as union, however gently expressed, with the Bishop of Rome.

There are many in the Anglican world who would go further than ask this question. Faced with Rome's charge that Anglican innovations might make a projected unity more difficult, even those in the Vatican most concerned with patrolling the boundaries must recognize that to many Anglicans it seems that this charge could be levelled the other way round. The dogmas relating to the papacy (1870) and to Mary (1950) remain real obstacles for many who find it difficult to recognize them as developments in any sense from scripture and the tenets of the Early Church, and the recent work of ARCIC has not managed to find a pathway to help the churches travel together in these areas. The *'filioque'* clause in the creed is to this day regarded by Eastern Orthodox Christians as an unwarranted Roman addition to the creed of the Universal Church. Anglicans will naturally ask by what criteria Rome claims the right to introduce potentially divisive innovations in some areas, while advising Anglicans against developing the practice, rather than altering the doctrine of the Church, in others. In what sense would ordaining women to the episcopate alter the doctrine of the Church? We note in this context that when Cardinal Kasper refers to Cyprian on the unity of the bishops he fails to point out that Cyprian was writing explicitly about the collegial unity of all bishops over against the possibility that the Bishop of Rome might tell the others what to do.

One of the most important points at which Cardinal Kasper seems to us to misrepresent the Anglican situation comes at the point where he indicates that he and others look to the Church of England as holding a place of decisive significance within Anglicanism, so that despite the fact that there are already women bishops in some provinces of the Anglican Communion the decision of the Church of England would somehow be key or crucial. That may be an accurate indication of how we are perceived, but the Church of England does not occupy the place in the Communion that the Vatican does in our sister church. Indeed, that imperial model – *Ecclesia Anglicana* telling the colonies how to behave – is precisely what we have done our best to avoid for several generations. As set out in the Windsor Report, we have a *modus operandi* according to which a potentially contentious issue can come to the Lambeth Conference, to the Anglican Consultative Council, and to the Primates' Meeting. To put it simply, if the Lambeth Conference gives a green light to a

114

proposal, it is then up to an individual province to decide whether to adopt any new development for itself. We must not for a moment collude with the impression that the Church of England occupies a position analogous to the Vatican and that the Lambeth Conference is merely an expensive piece of window-dressing. This tells heavily against the argument, sometimes advanced from within Anglicanism itself, that the decision we now face in the Church of England is the real defining moment. The Lambeth Conference has already given the green light to ordaining women to the episcopate; all we are being asked now is whether we, in our province, want to adopt for ourselves something to which worldwide Anglicanism has already given approval, and which can therefore not be seen within our own interprovincial polity as communion-breaking.

The question of Cardinal Kasper bringing a distinctively Roman perspective to Anglican affairs is also revealed in his remarks about unity, and about the role of the ordained ministry, and particularly of bishops, in engendering communion within that. The Anglican tradition takes its role as a 'bridge' seriously, and we too believe that we must work for, discern and enhance that unity for which Jesus prayed. But we do not believe that eucharistic unity ('communion' in that sense) is only attainable when there is full recognition of ministries, and all are in communion with the See of Rome. In Anglican theology, unity is achieved by our saying 'yes' to God's gracious invitation to his table. It is because we are one with God through being caught up in Christ's one perfect self-offering to the Father that we have unity with one another, rather than communion with God being a consequence of our union with one another. We, in other words, are inclined to see eucharistic sharing not as the goal at the end of the ecumenical pilgrimage where God is waiting for us, but as the path of that pilgrimage itself, along which he accompanies us on the way. We would base our theology of union within the Godhead on a dynamic incorporation into the divine life of the Holy Trinity, rather more than on a sacramental theology based on the validity of the sacrament confected by one who has the authority to do so; and we would prefer to see debates about orders within the frame of mutual eucharistic hospitality, rather than the other way around. In this regard, we would look to Galatians 2, with its clear teaching that all who believe in Jesus Christ belong at the same table, no matter what their cultural background.

There also needs to be further discussion on the nature of catholicity. A defining feature of the Church of the New Testament and the early centuries was that, unlike many other religious movements of the time, it was not based on race or profession. It broke through social but also natural divisions such as age and gender. It did this above all in its foundational, eucharistic life, as we learn from 1 Corinthians 11, and from that basis its total life was formed. The Church today in its local existence must continue to embrace people of a wide variety of different types and kinds, including people with diverse opinions. This is, indeed, what is constitutive of the Church's catholicity, as has amply been demonstrated by the Greek Orthodox theologian John Zizioulas, who writes:

> the eucharistic community was in its composition a *catholic community* in the sense that it transcended not only social but also natural divisions, just as it will happen in the Kingdom of God of which this community was a revelation and a real sign.[2]

The Augustinian understanding of catholicity as universal overtook the more ancient Pauline and Ignatian understanding of catholicity as inclusive. Wholeness is of the very essence of Church and without it the Church is not what she is called to be.

---

2   John Zizioulas, *Being as Communion* (London: Darton, Longman & Todd, 1985), p. 152. See also John Zizioulas, 'The Ecclesiological Presuppositions of the Holy Eucharist', in *Nicolaus* 10 (1982), pp. 333–49

In discussing the source of the Church's authority, the Cardinal comes close at times to saying that it is only through the lens of the Church's tradition that scripture can be read. That has never been the Anglican position on the balance between scripture and tradition. Our formulation, carefully balanced, is that the faith we profess is a faith 'uniquely revealed in the Holy Scriptures, set forth in the Catholic creeds, and to which the historic formularies of the Church of England bear witness'. Our formularies continue with this historically based mission imperative: 'the Church, ... led by the Holy Spirit, ... has borne witness to Christian truth in its historic formularies, the Thirty-Nine Articles of Religion, The Book of Common Prayer and the Ordering of Bishops, Priests and Deacons, ...and is called upon to proclaim [this faith] afresh in each generation.' This commitment to proclaim the faith afresh is a challenge to pursue those developments in the Church's life which are consonant with scripture and are found to be life-giving. In the end, the arbiter is the *sensus fidei*, the entire body of the faithful, as was pointed out to Pius IX in 1848 by the Eastern Patriarchs in their encyclical: 'the protector of religion is the very body of the Church, even the people themselves'. The faithful are the ultimate guardians of tradition and the faith.

Thus, while the Cardinal declares that the Roman Catholic Church is convinced that she has no authority for ordaining women, the Anglican Church would characteristically say that if this undoubted innovation can be shown to follow from, or be contained in, scripture, then that is sufficient authority whether or not the subsequent tradition of the Church has allowed it. This is not to be cavalier with tradition, to which we give a very high regard; merely to insist that (since, as Aquinas himself insisted, 'tradition' is the deposit of what the Church has said as it has read scripture) it must always take second place to scripture – the whole of the scriptural revelation and not just a selection of 'proof texts' – itself. This is the method which Anglicans have classically embraced, and which we attempt to follow as a fundamental theological method.

In short, while we respect the Cardinal's substantial analysis of where we are from a Roman perspective, and remain deeply grateful for the seriousness with which he takes his friendship with us, we wish to respond to that friendship in exactly the same way, by speaking frankly of the fact that his perception of how Anglicans might do theology is precisely a Roman perception, and that we perceive our theological method, and much that flows from it, in an authentically and characteristically Anglican way which needs to be taken seriously as what it is, rather than treated as if it were a muddled way of doing Roman-style theology.

### Women bishops: biblical exegesis and theological anthropology

Cardinal Kasper's reference to Junia in Rom. 16.7 itself seemed to allow that there might after all be a possibility of reopening the question; if, he seemed to imply, it could be demonstrated that Junia really was a woman (not 'Junias', a supposedly masculine name, as most translations have had it), then even Roman tradition might be forced to recognize the possibility that women could be apostles, and therefore presumably could hold ordained ministry in the apostolic succession. In fact, despite what the Cardinal suggested at that point in his paper, recent scholarship, drawing on excellent philology and study of ancient names, strongly suggests that the person in question was female. Junia is a well-known female name of the period, but the suggested male name Junias is not otherwise known; and, when Greek scribes began to introduce accents into their texts, they accented the name in such a way as to make it clear that it was female. That, despite what the Cardinal said, is how it appears in the most recent edition of the Nestlé–Aland Greek New Testament; and the newest edition of Metzger's commentary on textual variants indicates that those who still preferred the masculine accentuation did so simply on the grounds that they doubted whether a woman would be referred to as an 'apostle' – which precisely begs the methodological question.

This small but significant point opens the way for a consideration of some of the larger exegetical and theological issues. First, and most important, we must give great weight to the fact that all four evangelists, but especially John, place the testimony of the women, and especially Mary Magdalen, in prime position in their accounts of Easter. It is to these women, and particularly to Mary, that the risen Lord entrusts the good news, and not to the male apostles themselves. It cannot be overemphasized that this was hugely counterintuitive in the ancient world. Had the narratives been invented later, this would never have commended the account; had the evangelists had any doubt that women were to be regarded as primary witnesses of the resurrection, they would never have allowed such a story to remain in their texts. Yet there it is, in each gospel. If, with Paul, we regard 'apostleship' as primarily constituted by witness to the resurrection, Mary Magdalen is the 'apostle to the apostles', as indeed some Roman theologians have styled her.

This addresses the highly significant question of anthropology, rightly raised by various parties in the debate. The evangelists, again particularly but not exclusively John, present the resurrection of Jesus not as an isolated 'miracle' but as the beginning of God's new creation, God's renewal of the whole world. Within that, the roles of men and women are re-evaluated, not (to be sure) to make them identical or interchangeable in any and all respects, but to celebrate their complementarity, not least their complementary apostolic witness to Jesus' resurrection. The same point is visible in Acts, where it is remarkable how women are singled out both as co-equal recipients of the outpoured Spirit and also as co-equal sufferers of persecution (Acts 9.2, etc.), a telltale sign that they were community leaders in their own right.

Witness to the resurrection on one hand, and participation in the Spirit on the other, is the gospel foundation of all sacramental life. The question of what has been called 'sacramental assurance' is answered in the New Testament not by a theory about ministry – the New Testament is innocent of any explicit or developed linkage of ordained ministry and the sacraments – but by the fact that, with the resurrection of Jesus and the gift of the Spirit, the new creation has begun in which heaven and earth, and also present and future, now overlap. That is the ontological basis for sacramental assurance.

The biblical argument against the ordination (and, *a fortiori*, consecration) of women has tended to rest on a portfolio of texts often supposed to speak of 'headship' in a way that rules out women's ordination. In fact these texts – in 1 Corinthians 11 and 14, Ephesians 5, and 1 Timothy 2 – are by no means as clearly opposed to female ordination as their proponents usually make out. 'Headship' is in fact only mentioned in 1 Corinthians 11 (where it has to do with headgear worn while leading in worship – hardly an argument against women's public ministry) and Ephesians 5 (where it concerns the manner of mutual submission between husband and wife). The passage in 1 Corinthians 14, thought by some conservative textual critics on good manuscript evidence to be an interpolation, relates, even if original, not to ministry but to the good order of worship services in which, as in some Middle Eastern churches today, local women might not always understand the language of public worship and might be inclined to chat amongst themselves. The famous passage in 1 Timothy 2 does not mention 'headship', and can properly be read, within a context (Ephesus) where the mainstream religion was female-only, as a warning against allowing women to usurp the proper ministry of men. In fact, the primary exhortation of 1 Tim. 2.11 is 'let the women learn' (the Greek *manthano* means 'learn, especially by study), and is qualified with a phrase which can mean 'in silence' but equally 'at leisure': in other words, women must be given the space to study for themselves, an obviously revolutionary proposal in that age as in many subsequent ones, not least because, in Paul's world as in Jesus', to 'study' would not be for one's own benefit alone, but in order to become a teacher of others. These arguments, so briefly sketched, are of course too brief to be conclusive, but should indicate that those who support the ordination of women to priestly and episcopal ministry cannot be dismissed as treating scripture in a

cavalier fashion, or as indulging in an exercise in fancy herme-
neutical footwork to imply that the text is now unimportant.

A second strand relates to the foundation of the theology of
orders in christology, rather than in the examination of the
practice of the Early Church. The ordained ministry of the
Church does not simply fulfil useful functions of oversight,
leadership and service, such as are variously described in the
Epistles: rather the ordained ministry focuses in those ministers
the diaconal and priestly call of all God's people, a call that is
founded in their baptism. They become what Austin Farrer called
'walking sacraments'. In speaking of our baptism, Paul is clear
(Gal. 3.27, 28) there can be no division between male and female:
both have put on Christ. Which of the baptized then can represent
Christ in the ministerial orders of the Church, can stand in the
*imago Christi*? Can it be only men, or would that be to confuse the
universal Christ with the Jesus of history? There is a strong
argument to say that only a ministry open to both men and
women can properly represent Christ, who became, in the words
of the Nicene Creed, *anthropos* (human), not *aner* (male).

A third strand develops the theology of creation and the new
creation. The old dispensation has God creating human kind,
male and female in his image and likeness (Gen. 1.27). Men and
women have an equal dignity, and male and female are seen as
complementary. Thus far we travel together. But if complementarity means differentiation of the two sexes by function, as is
clearly expressed in Cardinal Kasper's paper, what does this have
to say about how men and women are together made in the image
and likeness of God? The true complementarity of the new
creation surely envisages men and women working together,
representing the unity of the divine image together in a way that
makes the kind of complementarity that Cardinal Kasper speaks
of look more like a kind of modalism. Certainly the place of the
Virgin Mary in the theology of the Victorines is more robust than
the traditionally passive one. When Hugh of St Victor describes
Mary's part in the birth of the Saviour in *De Sacramentis*, he says:

Nor is the Holy Spirit himself to be called the father of Christ because his love operated the conception of the virgin, since He did not contribute the seed to the foetus of His own essence to the virgin but provided substance to the Virgin herself from her own flesh through his love and virtue.

A further strand acknowledges the 'dynamic nature of tradition', and develops the notion of apostolicity in an eschatological direction, where it becomes more important to consider the Church's apostolic witness not just in terms of historical perspective but as a sign of a redeemed creation. If there is 'an apostolic procession to the end of time', then women and men have an equally significant contribution to make to the apostolic mission of the Church now, in the apostolic order.

## The faith as the Church of England has received it

The faith that the Church of England has received is, as already indicated, the apostolic faith uniquely revealed in Holy Scripture, set forth in the catholic creeds, and witnessed by our historic formularies, including the Ordinal. It focuses on Jesus himself, and his unveiling of the Father through his announcing of the kingdom and his death and resurrection, and on the sending of the Spirit through whom his followers are enabled to bear witness to him throughout the world. Announcing the Son in the power of the Spirit is the foundation of all Christian, new-covenant ministry. There is ample evidence in the earliest Christianity known to us that this ministry was shared by women. Nothing in holy scripture, the catholic creeds, or our historic formularies makes it necessary to go against this primal witness.

How we move forward in these matters is a question of appropriate and careful strategy, granted our calling to guard the unity of the Church. That we may, and indeed must, move forward is a conviction that can be reached, not on the basis of a casual or sloppy attitude to scripture and theology, nor in disregard for our ecumenical partners, but out of a deep conviction rooted in the gospel itself. It may be that the prophetic witness in this matter to which the Church of England is, we believe, called is a greater contribution to the unity of the whole people of God for which our Lord prayed so deeply.

# Epilogue: Recent Developments in the Women Bishops Debate

## MARK D. CHAPMAN

Since this book was first published as a special issue of the *Affirming Catholicism Journal* in 2006, the debate on women bishops in the Church of England has moved on relatively rapidly. This epilogue briefly describes the various stages of the debate. The report, *Women Bishops in the Church of England*, chaired by Michael Nazir-Ali, Bishop of Rochester, and published on 2 November 2004, presented a lengthy historical and theological account of the nature and development of episcopacy. It went on to discuss the theological and ecclesiological implications of the introduction of women bishops, before concluding with a number of possible options (§7). Although the possible repercussions of these different options were discussed, there were no specific recommendations about what to do next.

This meant that a second smaller group was appointed by the House of Bishops to discuss the choices and to make some proposals to General Synod about which option might best be suited for the current situation, that is, 'to offer ... its own considered assessment of where, out of the range of theoretical options, the real choice lay'.[1] This group was chaired by Christopher Hill, Bishop of Guildford, and comprised three episcopal colleagues: Pete Broadbent (Willesden); John Saxbee (Lincoln) and Nicholas Read (Blackburn). It also included one senior woman: Joy Tetley, Archdeacon of Worcester. Although a full consultation was not undertaken (since this would have been to repeat the work of the Rochester group), the Guildford group met nine times over the course of about a year and heard representations from different groups. It had received nearly 500 letters by the end of 2005. At the July 2005 Synod a motion was carried to 'set in train the process for removing the legal obstacles to the ordination of women to the episcopate'. Norman Russell, Archdeacon of Berkshire, added an amendment which asked the group to

---

1   House of Bishops Papers, HB (05) 12 §4.

give specific attention to the issues of canonical obedience and the universal validity of orders throughout the Church of England as it would affect clergy and laity who cannot accept the ordination of women to the episcopate on theological grounds.[2]

This gave the group greater focus, especially as it tried to work out plans for those opposed to the ordination of women as bishops. There was intense lobbying from various groups, many of which had produced official responses to the Rochester report.

After the Guildford group published its report in January 2006,[3] General Synod debated its draft tentative proposals for the accommodation of those opposed to the ordination of women as bishops. These were summarized under the heading 'Transferred Episcopal Arrangements' (TEA) (§§40–48). What was suggested was a 'provincial regional bishop' under the direct authority of the archbishop of the province, who would serve as 'ordinary'. At the February 2006 Synod it was suggested that this idea should be explored further. The Bishop of Guildford and Michael Perham, Bishop of Gloucester, were asked to make more specific proposals in the light of the many responses that had been received to the Guildford Report. In their document they suggested another form of oversight which would address some of the complexities of the TEA proposals, in particular the transfer of 'ordinary' jurisdiction from the diocesan bishop to the archbishop.[4] It was clear that having two 'ordinaries' within one diocese might well cause legal and administrative confusion, as well as making diocesan structures and planning highly problematic. Consequently, the Bishops of Guildford and Gloucester moved towards the idea of 'Shared Episcopal Oversight'. This proposal sought to guarantee

---

2    This is posted at: www.cofe.anglican.org/info/cofegazette/comms 2005/c0705.doc
3    General Synod Papers, GS 1605.
4    General Synod Papers, GS Misc. 826.

sufficient safeguards for those opposed to the ordination of women bishops, but at the same time ensure that ordinary jurisdiction (i.e., the highest legal authority), would be vested in the diocesan bishop, even though all pastoral and sacramental roles would be delegated.

Shortly before the July 2006 General Synod, Cardinal Walter Kasper, president of the Pontifical Council for Promoting Christian Unity, addressed the House of Bishops' meeting at Market Bosworth. Not surprisingly, he reiterated official Roman Catholic teaching on the ordination of women (that the Church has no authority to take such a decision), although he was obviously forced to admit that the Church of England had taken the step of ordaining women to the priesthood. He also noted that the sacrament of ordination was a single sacrament which meant that logically it should be possible to move from one stage to the next. Nevertheless, he regarded the ordination of women bishops as presenting new problems for ecumenical relations. His argument was practical rather than simply theological, and based principally on the sense of episcopal collegiality: the ordination of women as bishops would lead to a greater degree of schism and weaken episcopal collegiality. It should consequently be avoided:

> If ... the consecration of a bishop becomes the cause of a schism or blocks the way to full unity, then what occurs is something intrinsically contradictory. It should then not take place, or should be postponed until a broader consensus can be reached.

Cardinal Kasper was also clear that from his point of view the Church of England occupied a special position in the Anglican Communion, which meant that its decision to ordain women bishops would have a more profound effect on ecumenical relations than the decisions which had already been taken (and put into effect) by a number of other provinces. He concluded by issuing a less than veiled warning to the bishops:

It would, in our view, further call into question what was recognized by the Second Vatican Council (*Unitatis Redintegratio*, 13), that the Anglican Communion occupied 'a special place' among churches and ecclesial communities of the West. We would see the Anglican Communion as moving a considerable distance closer to the side of the Protestant churches of the sixteenth century. It would indeed continue to have bishops, according to the Lambeth Quadrilateral (1888); but as with bishops within some Protestant churches, the older churches of East and West would recognize therein much less of what they understand to be the character and ministry of the bishop in the sense understood by the early church and continuing through the ages.[5]

Despite this warning of increased Protestantism, however, the 2006 July General Synod voted

That this Synod welcome and affirm the view of the majority of the House of Bishops that admitting women to the episcopate in the Church of England is consonant with the faith of the Church as the Church of England has received it and would be a proper development in proclaiming afresh in this generation the grace and truth of Christ.

A second motion set in train the legislative process. Important amendments were added during the debate, which are shown in italics:

That this Synod, *endorsing Resolution III.2 of the Lambeth Conference 1998 'that those who dissent from, as well as those who assent to the ordination of women to the priesthood and*

---

5   This speech was published in full at: http://www.zenit.org/articl e-16339?l=english

*episcopate are both loyal Anglicans' and* believing that the implications of admitting women to the episcopate will best be discerned by continuing to explore in detail the practical and legislative arrangements:

(a) invite dioceses, deaneries and parishes to continue serious debate and reflection on the theological, practical, ecumenical and missiological aspects of the issue;

(b) invite the Archbishops' Council, in consultation with the Standing Committee of the House of Bishops and the Appointments Committee, to secure the early appointment of a legislative drafting group, *which will aim to include a significant representation of women in the spirit of Resolution 13/31 of the Anglican Consultative Council passed in July 2005*, charged with:

> (i) preparing the draft measure and amending canon necessary to remove the legal obstacles to the consecration of women to the office of bishop;
>
> (ii) preparing a draft of possible additional legal provision *consistent with Canon A4* to establish arrangements that would seek to maintain the highest possible degree of communion with those conscientiously unable to receive the ministry of women bishops;
>
> (iii) submitting the results of its work to the House of Bishops for consideration and submission to Synod; and

(c) instruct the Business Committee to make time available, before first consideration of the draft legislation, for the Synod to consider, in the light of any views expressed by the House of Bishops, the arrangements proposed in the drafting group's report.

The intention of the two significant amendments was twofold: first, to ensure that those who disagreed with the decision could nevertheless still be counted as loyal Anglicans and assured of a place in the Church of England; and, secondly, to guarantee the validity of the orders of those ordained deacon, priest or bishop, which is the implication of 'consistent with Canon A4'.

A third more representative group, chaired by Nigel McCulloch, Bishop of Manchester, has been set up to draft the legislation. This consists of Donald Allister, Archdeacon of Chester; Jonathan Baker, Principal of Pusey House; Sheila Cameron, Dean of the Arches; Vivienne Faull, Dean of Leicester; Dr Paula Gooder, a biblical scholar from the Queen's Foundation, Birmingham; Mrs Margaret Swinson; Sr Anne Williams (a Church Army sister and vice-chairman of Forward in Faith); and Trevor Willmott, Bishop of Basingstoke. Various representations have been heard from many different groups.

Although the ground has shifted and there is now talk of a 'free diocese' (rather than a third province) from some of the opponents, some stumbling-blocks remain. For those opposed these are focused particularly on the swearing of an oath to a woman ordinary, and for those in favour there are concerns about the dismantling of diocesan structures. Affirming Catholicism has played its full part in the debates and has made representations to the legislative drafting group which are currently being discussed. At present serious work is being undertaken on the nature of ordinary jurisdiction and oaths of canonical obedience, as well as the importance of exercising episcopacy in partnership with the synodical structures of the Church.

# Appendix:
## Documents for the Women Bishops debate produced by Affirming Catholicism

**Document 1: Letter from Richard Jenkins, Director of Affirming Catholicism to the Rt Revd Christopher Hill on Provision for those opposed to the admission of women to the Episcopate (3 November 2005)**

I am writing on behalf of the executive committee of Affirming Catholicism concerning the implementation of the Rochester Report, and in particular the issue of how to provide for those opposed to the ordination of women as bishops. For the reasons outlined below, we believe that the only acceptable way forward is a single clause measure with a code of practice coupled with the creation of a robust mechanism to ensure compliance to safeguard those who cannot accept women bishops.

*The proper parameters of the debate*

Your article published in September's *New Directions* gave a helpful insight into the House of Bishops' take on the main issues. In that article you suggested three possible ways in which the Church of England might proceed to admit women to the episcopate: a single-clause measure with a code of practice; a 'structural' approach which provided legislative safeguards for those who cannot accept women bishops; or the creation of a third province. However, by setting the parameters for discussion in this way, Affirming Catholicism believes that the debate has been skewed.

In fact the spectrum of options ranges from a single-clause measure without any provision to legislation to proceed with the creation of a third province. By not mentioning the former albeit radical option, the centre ground has been shifted towards a legislative approach for dealing with those who cannot accept the ministry of a woman bishop. This is not a sustainable solution.

We accept that for those who cannot accept women bishops the main issues are those of canonical obedience and jurisdiction, but we believe that *key issues which must also be addressed are the need to maintain the catholicity of the Church and to build trust.*

## Maintaining the catholicity of the Church

One of the catalysts for the formation of Affirming Catholicism was the need to defend the legitimacy of the ordination of women to the priesthood. We saw this and continue to see this as a scriptural and catholic development in tune with the liberating message at the heart of the Christian tradition, and the Christian understanding of humanity. We see no theological objection to the extension of women's ordained ministry to the episcopate and welcome the opening up of all forms of episcopal ministry to women on exactly the same terms as men.

Some question the authority of the Church of England to make such a decision unilaterally without the agreement of the Roman Catholic and Orthodox Churches, and have consequently not been able to accept this as a legitimate development.

- *While we understand this reasoning and the importance of ecumenism, we must point out that the admission of women to the episcopate does not create any new issue which the Church of England has not already dealt with in relation to the ordination of women to the presbyterate. Moreover, our continuing equivocation on the issue makes increasingly difficult our relationships with churches which have ordained women.*

We believe that the Church of England was established on the basis of the need to act unilaterally when the wider Church fails to act in accord with Catholic truth, and we hold to the principle so clearly enunciated by Michael Ramsey that 'Catholicism always stands before the Church door at Wittenberg to read the truth by which she is created and by which she is to be judged.' We are a reformed and reforming movement within the Church catholic.

When the Church discerns this call we must act with humility but also conviction. We affirm the ministry of women and believe in the legitimacy of the Church of England to decide on matters indifferent, among which we would include the gender of those who may be admitted to the ordained ministry of the Church. However, the ministry of the Church is not itself an indifferent matter: the threefold ministry is an effectual sign of our maintenance of the historic faith and a concrete expression of our being part of the universal Church.

In opening up the ordained ministry to women, it is crucial not to undermine the integrity of the ministry itself by creating a separate, parallel but less effectual 'woman minister'. This would be the case with any 'structural solution' involving legislation which, on the face of it, opened the episcopate to women, but with caveats, conditions and restrictions written into the measure. The effect of such legislation would be to create a separate class of 'woman bishop' alongside but not equal to male bishops in the scope of their ministry. This would be both discriminatory and uncatholic.

- *A legislative approach which sought to make provision for those who cannot accept the consecration of women by limiting the ministry of women bishops would bifurcate the episcopacy and rob it of both its symbolic and effective power, undermining profoundly the very threefold ministry we share with the rest of the universal Church and which we claim to maintain.*

This option is very likely to provoke strong resistance from those who believe that the time is right to admit women to the episcopate and who also believe that the Church of England is part of the one, holy catholic and apostolic Church.

133

*Oaths of obedience*

A year after women were ordained to the priesthood, the Act of Synod was passed and the extended episcopal oversight that it established has maintained some sort of unity between people holding different views about women's ordination. In most parts of the Church of England parishes which have opted for extended episcopal oversight are very small in number. However, while under the Act clergy have been able to make the oaths of canonical obedience to their diocesan bishops, they have also in practice been able to reject episcopal ministry from bishops who ordain women.

- *As we now contemplate how the Church can charitably accommodate those who cannot accept women as bishops we must not inadvertently de jure or de facto undermine the fullness of the ministry exercised as a class by women ordained to the episcopate even where individual parishes might receive extended episcopal care.*

We cannot see that a woman appointed as suffragan or assistant bishop would create any new difficulties except that some may not recognize deacons and priests ordained by her as validly ordained. These clergy would presumably not be invited to minister in a parish which had petitioned for extended oversight. Since numbers would be small it is unlikely that this would present many practical difficulties.

New issues arise for those opposed only where a woman was appointed as ordinary. It would be highly unlikely that a woman bishop would be appointed to a diocese where there were significant numbers opposed to her ministry. Nevertheless it is likely that in every diocese there would be some who would find it difficult to accept her authority. However, we do not feel that this is insurmountable.

It is quite possible for clergy to recognize a woman diocesan bishop as ordinary without thereby requiring her to minister pastorally or spiritually in their parishes. Under the present Act of Synod, an oath of canonical obedience to the diocesan bishop is consistent with extended episcopal oversight. And there are historical examples of lay people exercising the legal authority of the ordinary with no spiritual jurisdiction – for example the monarch in relation to Royal Peculiars.

Therefore, where a parish experiences particular difficulties because its diocesan bishop is a woman, she should still maintain legal responsibility for the exercise of ministry in the parish while nonetheless refraining from exercising direct pastoral or spiritual oversight. At a human level she would of course have continued pastoral concern for the cure of souls in that parish. This situation would be no more anomalous than the licensing of a woman priest to the cure of souls by a bishop who did not recognize the validity of her orders.

- *It would make a nonsense of the catholic understanding of the Church for clergy to make oaths of obedience to a bishop other than their diocesan. The catholicity and apostolicity of the Church are not the possession of single lines of bishops with certain views, but rather they belong to the whole Church. In making pastoral provision for the consciences of the few we must not lose this bigger picture.*

### Building trust and making provision for the minority

We recognize that there are those in the Church who do not believe that the Church should open the ministry to women. We respect their conscience and deeply value the spiritual gifts offered by those who remain opposed to the ordination of women. We do not seek to alienate them and we believe that it is possible to maintain for them a place in the life and ministry of the Church of England.

We appreciate the time now being taken to consider the nature and ramifications of such provision. When the Act of Synod was passed there had been no debate in the dioceses about the proposal, and the General Synod was not presented with any draft to consider, but required to vote on the Act over the space of two days, exactly one year after the substantive vote on the measure admitting women to the priesthood. We cannot repeat such hasty action.

We believe that the underlying issue in the current debate is that those who cannot accept the ministry of women bishops simply do not trust the institutions of the Church to deal with them fairly and consistently and in a way which guarantees their future in the Church. This is a tragic situation for which we must all take responsibility.

- *The way forward must be to build trust, to back up assurances of respect with robust systems to ensure that behaviour matches rhetoric and to maintain the maximum level of communion that is consistent with conscience.*

We do not believe that a third province is an adequate way of doing this. Apart from the fact that it would be small and ineffectual it is hard to see how it could seriously remain a part of the Church of England. It would mean that an important voice and tradition would be lost to the wider Church and it is likely that it would quickly resemble the continuing churches elsewhere with little effective mission and a lack of diversity. It would also undermine the parochial principle of the Church of England.

- *By creating 'no go' areas a third province would effectively erect an ecclesial 'peace wall' which would prevent dialogue and mutual enrichment. We must learn the lessons of secular history that partitions and peace walls do not solve conflict, nor ever adequately contain it.*

Instead we must look to a solution which does not divide us but which rather expresses mutual respect and promotes the dialogue and encounter which is at the core of our Anglican experience of *koinonia.* We suggest that a code of practice as outlined in §7.3.26 of the Rochester Report would give concrete expression to the real concern most members of the Church feel to safeguard the position of those who cannot accept women as bishops, but without undermining fundamental ecclesiological principles which are crucial to our catholicity, apostolicity and unity. By avoiding the creation of a church within a church it would allow dialogue and common life to continue between those who have different views on the place of women in the ordained ministry but who otherwise share the same gospel, mission and tradition.

However, we recognize that those who oppose the ordination of women feel a very real lack of confidence and trust in the Church and that a code of practice in and of itself is not likely to provide the measure of protection they feel they need.

They fear that over time bishops will feel less bound by its provisions and that even in the short term different bishops will take quite different approaches to applying the code within their diocese, or that a bishop with whom they have a good relationship might be succeeded by someone less sympathetic. These are real concerns which must be addressed.

- *We recommend that a code of practice must be backed up by a mechanism at national level to ensure consistency and compliance across the country. Such a mechanism might be a panel of reference under the aegis of the Archbishops, set up to monitor implementation of the code and to investigate particular breaches. In making this recommendation we have in mind the parallel of the recently set up Communion-wide panel of reference.*

The panel would report to the Archbishops and House of Bishops but also publish annually its findings, so that the whole Church can be informed about the level of care being shown to those of a minority view. Mediation and arbitration, in line with the provisions of the code, should also be made available at provincial level, and similarly monitored and reported on by the panel. We believe that a code of practice, backed up by such a mechanism to ensure compliance, would give the appropriate measure of protection to those who oppose the ordination of women without compromising basic principles of catholic order.

*Conclusion*

Affirming Catholicism therefore supports the first option of the Rochester Report: a simple, single clause allowing women to proceed to episcopal ministry but with the significant addition of a robust mechanism to ensure consistent compliance. At the same time, while we believe that it is vitally important that Christian charity is shown towards those who in good conscience cannot accept the ministry of a woman bishop, such pastoral provision must not undermine the fullness of the episcopal ministry exercised by women. That would be discriminatory to individual women bishops, and it would undermine the catholicity and apostolicity of the whole Church.

**Document 2: Developing the proposals in the Guildford Report: A submission by the Executive Committee of Affirming Catholicism (2 April 2006).**[1]

*Introduction*

1. During the General Synod debate on the Guildford Group's Report, the Bishop of Southwark made the following contribution:

> I am one of those Catholic Anglicans who believe that the ordination of women as priests and indeed as bishops is a legitimate development of Catholic Church order and ministry, whereas I fear that TEA risks leading us to be a Church which departs in many significant ways from Catholic Church order and practice. We could end up with the anomalous situation of a Church so un-Catholic that no Catholic Anglican, whatever their position on women's ordination, would wish to belong.[2]

2. In the light of these concerns, which we share, Affirming Catholicism has prepared this contribution to the 'further exploration' asked for by Synod. Whilst eagerly awaiting the ordination of women to the episcopate, we are equally committed to the catholic tradition within the Church of England. We

---

1   The members of the Affirming Catholicism working party were the Revd Jonathan Clarke (chair of the working party; Rector of St Mary's Stoke Newington, Rector of the Society of Catholic Priests); the Revd Dr Mark Chapman (Vice-Principal, Ripon College, Cuddesdon, Oxford); the Revd Richard Jenkins (Director, Affirming Catholicism): Mrs Mary Johnston (Chair of the Steering Group of Affirming Catholicism in General Synod); the Revd Dr Charlotte Methuen (Departmental Lecturer in Ecclesiastical History, Faculty of Theology, University of Oxford).

2   Proceedings, 9 February 2006, p. 24.

believe that the TEA (Transferred Episcopal Arrangements) proposals as they stand do not in some key respects reflect the principle expressed in the chairman's Note on Sacramental Assurance that

> whatever private reservations some may feel obliged to take in relation to women bishops and those ordained by them, the proper provision and space the church should make for those who are opposed must fall short of officially raising doubt about any ordinations in the Church (§130).

3. We are particularly concerned that the manner in which the provision of alternative episcopal oversight is envisaged institutionalizes doubt within the Church concerning its own ministry.[3] It thus undermines the foundational role of the diocese, and of diocesan structures, in the ministry and mission of an episcopally ordered church. To proceed with the TEA proposals unamended would undermine the catholic order of the Church in such a profound way that we would share the Bishop of Southwark's doubts about our continued claim to share in that order.

4. The Guildford group were naturally (given the resolution passed by Synod last July) concerned with the situation of those who are opposed to the ordination of women to the episcopate. On that basis, they proposed the London [diocese] plan as a model for moving forward which could create 'a form of shared

---

3    It may of course be argued that the provision of the Act of Synod that 'the integrity of differing beliefs and positions concerning the ordination of women to the priesthood should be mutually recognized and respected' already allows for such non-recognition of ministries. We would argue that any such non-recognition is at the level of personal belief and therefore does not – and must not – compromise the Church's belief that all those duly ordained are ordained and should be recognized as such by all (Canon A4).

episcopal ministry' (§44). The point of the London plan, however, was to maintain the integrity of the diocese.[4] We believe that by translating the London plan to provincial level, Guildford compromises that key ecclesial principle of catholic order. However, we also believe that Guildford's fundamental premise and many of its recommendations offer a constructive way forward.

5. In developing the proposals of the Guildford Report we turned our attention firstly to the question the group posed itself: *What is needed to enable women to be fully accepted in the threefold ministry of deacons, priests and bishops?* (§16). Our response is that, if the Church is to ordain women to the episcopate, it should not be done apologetically but in confidence and thankfulness to God. Our proposals for taking forward the Guildford report therefore come under three headings: joyful acceptance, recognition and reception.

*Joyful acceptance*

6. We accept the competence of the Church of England, working through its proper Synodical processes, to make decisions for the ordering of its life. As the Roman Catholic observer to General Synod commented in his contribution to the presentation of ecumenical responses to the Rochester report: 'From our perspective at least, either it is right and you do it, or it is wrong and you do not do it, or we do not know yet and so we need to study further in order to decide whether to do it or not.'[5] If the Church does take this step, it should do so in confidence that it is making the right decision. For this reason (see below) we do not accept the concept of 'open reception' that has been relied upon in

---

4    In Section 4 of the London plan the bishops acknowledge the function of the Bishop of London as ordinary and as the focus of unity within the diocese. See: http://www.bishopoffulham.co.uk/Declaration.htm

5    Proceedings, 6 February 2006, p. 13.

relation to recent divisions within the Church concerning women's ministry.

7. The key structural principle that we believe must remain unimpaired, if the ministry of women in the episcopate is to be accepted within the Church of England, is that also enunciated in the first clause of the Act of Synod: 'The bishop of each diocese continues as the ordinary of his [sic] diocese'.[6] As the Guildford Report states, we must maintain an 'ecclesiological balance between clarity and charity' (§37). It is our contention that this balance must be struck by allowing maximum scope for conscientious dissent within this fundamental principle, even to the extent of allowing arguably a wider range of discrimination on the grounds of gender than the Guildford Report permits.

8. A degree of diversity is core to Anglican ecclesiology: we believe that we are as a body enriched by including people with different views, even on key issues of Christian faith. Catholic order is shown not so much in the enforcement of uniformity as in the inclusion of diversity, but it must also provide a boundary within which that diversity can flourish. That boundary, encompassing the maximum of diversity whilst also bringing believers together as one body, seems to be best expressed in the notion of the Church in the diocese as the core unit of ecclesial life. We wish then to see remaining within the same local church, as fully as possible, and under the bishop as ordinary, those who hold differing views on this as on other issues. Within that context we believe that 'reception' can continue through a process of dialogue and encounter across permeable borders.

9. We recognize that a minority within the Church continue to have private reservations about women's ministry, and we have no desire to see them excluded on those grounds. (We recognize also that this restriction on their ministry causes pain to many women priests.) But the Church of England has learned to live

---

6    http://www.bishopoffulham.co.uk/Act%20of%20Synod.htm

with those reservations and we suggest that the kind of structures we propose can continue to provide for conscientious dissent.

*Recognition*

10. All those who are canonically ordained in the Church of England, regardless of their gender or the gender of their ordaining bishops, are to be regarded as competent to fulfil all the duties of whatever post to which they have been appointed. Clearly this means that there can be no question of re-ordination (or indeed re-confirmation).

11. Taking this fundamental principle together with the premise that the diocese is the basic unit of mission and ministry in the Church, the integrity and structures of which must be preserved, we propose that provision for those who have private reservations about the episcopal ministry of women should take the form of *shared*, rather than transferred, episcopal arrangements.

12. We propose that a system along the lines of that outlined in Guildford will work best if the bishop exercising shared episcopal authority clearly acts as an area bishop within the diocese, sharing the oversight of parishes in his care with the diocesan and acting in consultation with and on behalf of the Diocesan as a member of Senior Staff and according to Diocesan policies and practices. Although it is envisaged that the continued appointment of bishops analogous to the present Provincial Episcopal Visitors (PEVs) will be required, licensed as now by the Archbishop, some dioceses may as at present wish to make provision by regional or intradiocesan appointments.

13. Bishops so appointed will always exercise sacramental ministry within parishes requesting it, but the other aspects of episcopal jurisdiction will be negotiated and shared out between the bishops working together as pastors in one Church, in order to ensure the highest degree of encounter and enrichment possible. Although Guildford (§22) says that those opposed to the ordination of women bishops could not accept any such arrangement because it would entail acceptance of women

bishops, we do not believe that this situation is any more anomalous than the position of bishops currently unable to accept the ordination of women who nevertheless install, license and receive oaths of obedience from women priests.

*Providing certainty and security of provision – how we should legislate*

14. We recognize nevertheless that those unable to accept the ordination of women bishops require provision with the greatest degree of certainty and security possible within this framework. *We therefore propose that the Measure admitting women to the episcopate contain a clause conferring a power on Synod to make regulations to provide a system of shared episcopal oversight for those unable to accept women bishops, along the lines set out below.* We expect that most aspects of the system will be created by the regulations but some items may be reserved for a code of practice – for example the nature of consultation which should take place before a Special Parochial Church Meeting (SPCM). We agree with the Guildford Group that breach of the regulations should constitute an offence against the laws ecclesiastical, subject to proceedings under the Clergy Discipline Measure (§88). The regulations should be drafted simultaneously with and voted on by Synod at the same time as the main measure.

15. Conversely, the legislation should also require a diocesan bishop who has made a declaration that he would take part neither in the ordination of women priests nor the consecration of women bishops to appoint an assistant bishop (who has not made such declarations) to assist him in the selection, training and ordination of women candidates for the ordained ministry, and their appointment, licensing and pastoral care. The assistant bishop would be a member of the senior staff of the diocese.

*The jurisdiction of bishops appointed under Shared Episcopal Arrangements (SEA)*

16. Should a parish request alternative oversight, the diocesan bishop shall be required to trigger the provision of ministry by a

provincial regional bishop or other bishop who has made a declaration that he would take part neither in the ordination of women priests nor the consecration of women bishops by authorizing him to exercise sacramental care and to share the pastoral and disciplinary functions of the diocesan bishop in respect of such parishes. The bishop so appointed (henceforth 'SEA bishop') would exercise a jurisdiction like that of an area bishop and would be a member of the senior staff of the diocese (§§ 41, 42, 116).

17. As area bishop, the SEA bishop would exercise sacramental ministry in the parish and would share pastoral care, ministerial review and disciplinary oversight of the clergy according to diocesan practice and policies.

18. The SEA bishop would act on behalf of the diocesan in relation to appointments by liaising with parishes in respect of vacancies and making recommendations for appointments to the diocesan bishop/board of patronage (§§ 43, 120).

19. The SEA bishop would oversee the selection, training and ordination of such candidates for ministry as have requested his oversight, making recommendations to the diocesan about the sponsorship of specific candidates in accordance with diocesan practice and policies. Ordinands would be part of the national system of selection and training (§§43, 124).

20. The SEA bishop would have power to initiate proposals in relation to pastoral measures within agreed diocesan strategies and policies and, as a member of the senior staff of the diocese, would have full voting rights in relation to parishes under his oversight and would be required to cooperate in any planning for mission and pastoral care (§43).

*Parishes seeking to come under the provisions of SEA*

21. Parishes could opt either to decline the ministry of a woman priest, or express their wish to receive the oversight of a SEA bishop by means of a two-thirds majority at a SPCM in favour of the relevant resolution(s) (§§98, 113). Every member of the

electoral roll should have been given notice of and consulted about the resolutions before the meeting according to good practice which should be set out in a code of practice. The diocesan bishop should meet with the Parish before the SPCM. Motions would be reviewed every five years and at every vacancy (§98). In the event that a parish wished only to consider resolutions 1 and/or 2 below, the obligation to consult with the diocesan bishop would not apply.

22. Clergy in such parishes would make oaths to the SEA bishop as area bishop *and* to the diocesan. Oaths would be administered by the SEA bishop. This is current practice in dioceses with an area system such as London where resolution 'C' parishes make oaths of canonical obedience to the Bishop of London and the Bishop of Fulham instead of their Area Bishop.[7]

*The office of Archbishop of Canterbury*

23. It seems sensible to give the Crown Nominations Commission statutory authority in relation to the See of Canterbury, to take into account the acceptability, across the Anglican Communion, at the time of appointment, of a woman archbishop.

*Reception*

24. The Rochester Report in its consideration of reception quotes Yves Congar:

> By reception we mean the process by which a church tradition appropriates a truth which has not arisen out of that tradition, but which it yet recognizes and adopts as a formulation of the faith. In the process of reception we understand something other than that which the

---

7   London Plan, §9: Any oaths to be taken to the Bishops of Stepney, Kensington, Willesden, Edmonton and Fulham at ordination to the priesthood, institution or licensings [*sic*] will also be taken to the Bishop of London as ordinary. See: http://www.bishopofful ham.co.uk/Declaration.htm

Scholastics meant by obedience. For them, this was the
act whereby a subordinate regulated his will and his
conduct according to the legitimate precepts of a
superior, out of respect for his/her authority. Reception is
not merely the expression of the relationship *secundum et
supra*; it includes the active giving of assent, even the
exercise of judgement, where the life of a body which
draws upon its original spiritual resources is expressed.[8]

25. We find this conception of reception necessary to a catholic
view of the church. To quote again the Roman Catholic observer
to Synod:

> There are some things about which we can sometimes
> say that it really does not matter who thinks what; there
> are other things about which we can say that we do think
> it matters but we can disagree without actually upsetting
> the fundamental structure. When it comes to the issue of
> order, because that affects the fundamental structure,
> then it is difficult to see, from our perspective, how there
> can be this understanding of provisionality.
>
> This is where we find it – I have to admit – difficult
> to understand precisely what is meant by an open process
> of reception, especially inside a particular communion:
> how some can say it is possible and some can say it is not
> possible.[9]

26. As Congar points out, reception need not entail passive
obedience to a command, even when the decision itself is not in
question. There is an active process whereby the Church exercises
judgement and discernment in what a decision made by the

---

8   Yves Congar 'Reception as an Ecclesiological Reality', in
    G. Alberigo and A. Weiler (eds), *Election and Consensus in the Church*,
    *Concilium* 77 (New York: Herder & Herder, 1972), p. 45.
9   Proceedings, 6 February 2006, p. 13.

Church means. Reception is not validation, but a process by which a decision is incorporated into the life of the Church.

27. Reception in this sense means that the Church of England is discerning how women might be received fully into the threefold ministry of the Church. In that context it is significant that over 50 per cent of ordinands in training for ordination are women. In all our structures we have to maintain the highest degree of permeability and reciprocity at every level to facilitate the process of learning and growing together. We therefore propose the following further provisions.

*Resolutions*

28. We recommend that the suggested resolutions (§113) should be amended as follows:

29. A two-thirds majority of a SPCM may pass one or more of the following resolutions:

> 1. That this parish would not accept a woman as the minister who presides or celebrates at Holy Communion or pronounces the Absolution in the parish.
> 2. That this parish would not accept a woman as the incumbent of the parish.
> 3. That this parish requests that, in the event of a woman being appointed as bishop of the diocese, arrangements for the sharing of episcopal ministry be made with a bishop who has made such declarations.
> 4. That this parish requests that, in the absence of any declaration by the bishop of the diocese for the time being that he would take part neither in the ordination of women priests nor the consecration of women bishops, arrangements for the sharing of episcopal ministry be made with a bishop who has made such declarations.

30. In parishes which had passed only resolutions 1 or 2 a woman bishop, while exercising all other episcopal functions, would respect the wishes of the parish in relation to sacramental ministry and appoint a male substitute. A SEA bishop would be nominated only in the event of resolution 3 or 4 being passed. This would allow parishes to continue to have the option of barring women from exercising a sacramental ministry and/or being licensed as incumbent of the parish, without automatically coming under the jurisdiction of a SEA bishop.

31. Although this would perpetuate the possibility of discrimination across the whole Church, we believe that the proposal to force all dissenting parishes into the jurisdiction of a SEA bishop would do violence to the variety of views across the Church, and much diminish the chance of any process of reception within the Church as a whole.

*Conclusion*

32. There are clearly other issues which do not require legislation which remain to be resolved, and will need to be covered in a code of practice or similar document. These include (though there will be many others): whether candidates at interview should ordinarily be asked about their views on women's ministry; the role of deans of women's ministry; the cases of multi-parish benefices in which one parish is opposed to the ministry of women. We do not underestimate the difficulty in producing workable legislation even though we hope that we have provided a more stable basis for it; and if we may be of further help to the working party we would welcome the opportunity to make a further contribution.

33. It has been our aim in producing this paper to resolve some of the contradictions inherent in the proposals of the Guildford Group. In the tension between ecclesiological clarity and charity, theological principle must be valued as much as the satisfaction of different parties. We hope that by our restatement of basic catholic principles we have been able to indicate a workable

structure whereby the ministry of women in the episcopate might be welcomed by the Church and the thinking of the Guildford Report constructively developed.

### Note on sacramental assurance by Charlotte Methuen

1. We note the helpful Appendix 2 on sacramental assurance by the Bishop of Guildford, to which we would wish to append the following points.

2. In some churches which ordain women to the priesthood, the argument of sacramental assurance has been used to support the move towards ordination of women with no provision made for those who are opposed.

3. In the Lutheran Church of Schaumburg-Lippe, the last of the Germany's *Landeskirchen* to introduce the ordination of women, it was decided that this decision should also mark the end of ordaining those opposed. The bishop, Jürgen Johannesdotter, explained the reason: 'We wanted every parish member to be sure that they were receiving true sacraments, absolution and blessing from every pastor ordained by the Church.' Here is a clear principle that sacramental assurance is maintained, not by any individual, whether parishioner or bishop, but by the Church and the decision of the Church.

4. A similar argument was used in the Old Catholic Church in Germany. Here the language used was that of intention: the Church required of its members, lay and ordained, that whatever their personal misgivings, they recognize all priests ordained by the Old Catholic Church in Germany and acknowledge their intention to celebrate sacraments, pronounce absolution and give the blessing. Those who have private misgivings nevertheless receive when the celebrant is a woman, for the intention to offer a eucharist has been affirmed by the Church. Again, sacramental assurance is held to be the responsibility of the Church.

5. To make sacramental assurance dependent upon the conscience of the individual, or even on the collective conscience of a particular congregation is to betray this principle. Language

suggesting that it is for a congregation to describe which bishop is 'acceptable' to them is ecclesiologically highly problematic. So too is the suggestion that a bishop must be subject to 'recognition' to individuals or congregations. To shift the foundation of sacramental assurance from the Church to the individual or parish is to betray the principle, summed up in the chairman's note, that 'assurance is given because this sacramental ministry does not depend upon personal feelings or individual dispositions but on the corporate, formal, act of the Church'.

**Document 3: A Submission to the Women Bishops Legislative Drafting Group of the General Synod of the Church of England by the Standing Committee of Affirming Catholicism (30 March 2007)[1]**

---

**Where we are now – a case study**

The incumbents of three neighbouring parishes are supposed to be working together. In two of the parishes resolutions A and B are in force; one is under extended episcopal oversight. However, while the incumbents of those parishes, R and S, are both opposed to the ordination of women as priests, the incumbent of the neighbouring parish, T, is in favour and in fact has a woman curate, U.
How do they work together?

For R, the fact that T has concelebrated with women priests precludes the possibility of any eucharistic concelebration, or even of his receiving the sacrament from T. S, on the other hand, sees no difficulty in sharing ministry with T, and has indeed attended a Eucharist at which U has presided, where he received her blessing. T will happily work with all his colleagues, and U would be glad to do so.

U will be moving on soon to her first incumbency, and is currently arranging a date for institution and licensing with her bishop, Z, who does not himself ordain women to the priesthood, but is prepared to license U to an incumbency in which she shares with him the cure of souls.

---

1    Submitted by the Standing Committee of Affirming Catholicism: the Revd Canon Nerissa Jones, MBE (Chair of Trustees); the Revd Dr Barry Norris (Chair of the Executive Committee); Mr Robin Welton (Treasurer); The Revd Richard Jenkins (Director)

*Introduction*

Affirming Catholicism believes that this case-study illustrates the complexity of the current situation which has arisen within the Church of England since the Priests (Ordination of Women) Measure 1993 and the arrangements made through the General Synod Episcopal Ministry Act of Synod 1993 came into force.

U and T – who may stand here for all those who accept the ministry of priests who are women – recognize and affirm the priestly ministry of their colleagues who are opposed. S wishes that the Church of England had not decided to ordain women as priests, but recognizes that the Church has in fact ordained U, although he prefers not to receive the Eucharist from her. R, like his Bishop Z, struggles with the question of whether U is ordained at all. For S, T and U and Bishop Z, the Church of England's Canon A4 stands, though S disagrees with the decision to ordain women to the priesthood, and Z has private doubts about the validity of women's priestly orders. R, however, would argue that Canon A4 is to some extent no longer in force.

As the Church of England admits women to the episcopate, Affirming Catholicism will be arguing in this submission – as we did in May 2006 – for a substantially similar set of pastoral arrangements to those made in 1993. However, as the debate around women bishops has progressed, it has become increasingly clear that it will be necessary in that legislation to delineate more clearly the limits of diversity within the Church of England. The question is: what can be provided for? That is, what level of dissent from the decisions of the Church of England can the Church of England reasonably be expected to allow?

The motion passed by the General Synod in July 2006 has sharpened the focus on this question. After further consideration and for the reasons set out below, we believe that it is possible – and, indeed, positively desirable in preserving the catholicity of the Church – to offer pastoral provision for those who dissent from the decision to admit women to the episcopate in the sense that they may wish that it had not happened, or that they believe that this is not the right time. However, by the same token, we contend that it is not possible to offer provision for those who wish to be insulated altogether from the fact of the ordained ministry of women because they believe that the Church of England has not made, or is not able to make, that decision. Specifically, we conclude that it would be simply impossible to contain within one church those who hold that women have been ordained bishop in the Church of England, and those who believe that those ordinations are not genuine. We believe that provision can and should be made for all those who accept the Church's decision but retain their private doubts, but cannot be made for those who regard that decision as null and void and who wish to live apart from the rest of the Church.

## *The decision of General Synod in July 2006*

In July 2006, the General Synod of the Church of England passed two motions relating to the admission of women to the episcopate. Although the motion passed in July 2005[2] had been

---

2    The following motion was passed by the General Synod in July 2005:

'That this Synod

(a) consider that the process for removing the legal obstacles to the ordination of women to the episcopate should now be set in train;

(b) invite the House of Bishops, in consultation with the Archbishops' Council, to complete by January 2006, and report to the Synod, the assessment which it is making of the various options for achieving the removal of the legal obstacles to the ordination of women to the episcopate, and ask that it give specific attention to the issues of canonical obedience and the universal validity of orders throughout the Church of England as it would affect clergy and laity who cannot accept the ordination of women to the episcopate on theological grounds; and

(c) instruct the Business Committee to make sufficient time available in the February 2006 group of sessions for the Synod to debate the report, and in the light of the outcome to determine on what basis it

widely heralded as opening the way for the consecration of
women as bishops in the Church of England, it was felt by some
to be somewhat half-hearted in its affirmation of the admission of
women to the episcopate and by others not to give a clear
statement that women could be admitted to the episcopate at all.
In their report to the House of Bishops, the Bishops of Guildford
and Gloucester concluded that the General Synod must be given
an opportunity unambiguously to state its acceptance of the
theological principles underlying the admission of women to the
episcopate, and the first motion to be discussed by General Synod
in July 2006 was explicitly presented to Synod by its presidents as
enabling a decision on 'the issue of substance'.[3]

> That this Synod welcome and affirm the view of the
> majority of the House of Bishops that admitting women
> to the episcopate in the Church of England is consonant
> with the faith of the Church as the Church of England
> has received it and would be a proper development in
> proclaiming afresh in this generation the grace and truth
> of Christ.

The motion was intended to allow Synod to state its acceptance of
the principle of admitting women to the episcopate. Its passing
indicates that in the mind of the majority – in both the House of
Bishops and the General Synod – there is no theological objection
to the consecration of women as bishops. It is thus rightly

---

wants the necessary legislation prepared and establish the necessary
drafting group.'

3   'In order to make progress, there needs now to be clarity on the issue
of substance. Is the admission of women to the episcopate in the
Church of England judged to be consonant with the faith of the
Church as the Church of England has received it and would it be a
proper development in proclaiming afresh in this generation the
grace and truth of Christ?' 'Women In The Episcopate: Note By The
Presidents', in General Synod Papers (GS 1630 §§7–8).

understood as a vote in favour of the principle of admitting women to the episcopate of the Church of England.

The second motion set in train the process for making that possible. This motion, passed by Synod with three amendments (shown in the following text in italics), read:

> That this Synod, endorsing Resolution 111.2 of the Lambeth Conference 1998 'that those who dissent from, as well as those who assent to the ordination of women to the priesthood and episcopate are both loyal Anglicans' and believing that the implications of admitting women to the episcopate will best be discerned by continuing to explore in detail the practical and legislative arrangements:
>
> (a) invite dioceses, deaneries and parishes to continue serious debate and reflection on the theological, practical, ecumenical and missiological aspects of the issue;
>
> (b) invite the Archbishops' Council, in consultation with the Standing Committee of the House of Bishops and the Appointments Committee, to secure the early appointment of a legislative drafting group, *which will aim to include a significant representation of women in the spirit of Resolution 13/31 of the Anglican Consultative Council passed in July 2005*, charged with:
>
> (i) preparing the draft measure and amending canon necessary to remove the legal obstacles to the consecration of women to the office of bishop;
>
> (ii) preparing a draft of possible additional legal provision *consistent with Canon A4* to establish arrangements that would seek to maintain the highest possible degree of communion with those conscientiously unable to receive the ministry of women bishops;
>
> (iii) submitting the results of its work to the House of Bishops for consideration and submission to Synod; and

(c) instruct the Business Committee to make time available, before first consideration of the draft legislation, for the Synod to consider, in the light of any views expressed by the House of Bishops, the arrangements proposed in the drafting group's report.

The motion expresses Synod's acknowledgement that legislation should include reasonable provision for those who are opposed to this move – thus recognizing them as 'loyal Anglicans' – but must at the same time ensure that such provision does not cast doubt upon the orders of deacons, priests and bishops who are women – that is, such legal provision must be 'consistent with Canon A4'.

### 'Consistent with Canon A4'

It is evident that the extent of the legal provision to be made to those who feel that they cannot in conscience accept the admission of women to the episcopate hangs to some extent on the interpretation of Canon A4.

A4 *Of the Form and Manner of Making, Ordaining, and Consecrating of Bishops, Priests, and Deacons*

The Form and Manner of Making, Ordaining, and Consecrating of Bishops, Priests, and Deacons, annexed to The Book of Common Prayer and commonly known as the Ordinal, is not repugnant to the Word of God; and those who are so made, ordained, or consecrated bishops, priests, or deacons, according to the said Ordinal, are lawfully made, ordained, or consecrated, and ought to be accounted, both by themselves and others, to be truly bishops, priests, or deacons.

As implied above, the amendment was moved with the intention of safeguarding the recognition of the orders of those lawfully ordained according to the Ordinal of the Church of England, who 'ought to be accounted, both by themselves and others, to be truly bishops, priests and deacons'.[4] The origins of Canon A4 shed light on the sense in which lawfully ordained bishops, priests and deacons 'ought to be accounted' to be such: in line with the 1603/4 Canon, this phrase has the implication 'are to be accounted [such] on pain of excommunication'. In practical terms, the impact of Canon A4 is: 'The Church says this, and you must do all you can to conform your conscience to the mind of the Church.' In this, the canon reflects the traditional catholic understanding that a person is properly ordained only if they are a legitimate candidate who has been ordained by a correct and authorized rite.[5] At the same time, the Church of England has a long tradition of recognizing some freedom of conscience within the obedience required 'in all things lawful and honest'.

The amendment thus demands that provision for those who feel themselves in conscience unable to accept the ministry of a bishop who is a woman may not call her orders into question. By extension, the orders of priests who are women may also not be placed in question. In other words, sacramental assurance is ensured by the Church and by the act of the Church, and not decided upon by any individual, whether parishioner or bishop. To make sacramental assurance dependent upon the conscience of the individual, or even on the collective mind of a particular congregation, is to betray this core catholic principle. As the

---

4   We are aware that it has been suggested that the reference to Canon A4 cannot bear the weight here placed upon it, although this interpretation was clearly in the mind of the amendment's proposer. For a more detailed consideration, see Appendices C and D.

5   This principle is enshrined also in Roman Catholic Canon Law through Canon 1009, §2: 'Orders are conferred by an imposition of hands and by the consecrating prayer which the liturgical books prescribe for the individual grades.' The same principle underlies the Roman Catholic declaration 'that Ordinations conferred according to the Edwardine rite should be considered null and void' (*Apostolicae Curae*, §15). The Roman Catholic view of Anglican orders as null and void thus rests upon the Roman Catholic teaching that the Anglican rite of ordination is defective.

Bishop of Guildford has noted, '[sacramental] assurance is given because this sacramental ministry does not depend upon personal feelings or individual dispositions but on the corporate, formal, act of the Church'.[6]

We believe that the measures already in place – the code of practice associated with the Priests (Ordination of Women) Measure 1993 and the arrangements made through the General Synod Episcopal Ministry Act of Synod 1993 – were intended to make arrangements for those who felt themselves in conscience unable to accept the ordination of women to the priesthood without calling into question the orders of those women. That is, Canon A4 was not annulled or qualified by those measures. The Church of England ordains women to the priesthood and expects those women to be viewed as legally, legitimately and validly ordained: 'they ought to be accounted, both by themselves and others, to be truly ... priests, or deacons'. Whilst the Act of Synod referred to the need for 'discernment in the wider Church of the rightness or otherwise of the Church of England's decision to ordain women to the priesthood', that discernment does not imply doubt about the orders of those women who have been lawfully ordained. The language of provisionality and reception does not imply that the orders of any particular woman are any more or less provisional than those of her male colleagues. In the extremely unlikely event that the Church of England were to conclude that its decision was not right, it would cease to ordain further women to the priesthood, but those already ordained could not be 'unordained', although they might be requested to refrain from exercising that ministry.[7]

---

6   Guildford Report, §130.

7   This was the procedure in the case of Florence Li Tim Oi, who was ordained priest in 1944 in an ordination which was subsequently declared to be illegitimate. As a result of that decision, Florence Li Tim Oi agreed not to exercise a priestly ministry. However, she was not re-ordained when women were admitted to the priesthood in Hong Kong in 1971. A similar procedure currently pertains when

Legislation that is 'consistent with Canon A4' thus requires that the women whom the Church of England has ordained as priests and deacons, and whom it in the future will consecrate as bishops, be recognized as such. Affirming Catholicism believes that legislation which is consistent with Canon A4 must therefore affirm the principle that every bishop, regardless of gender, is a bishop. Consequently, every diocesan bishop, regardless of gender, must continue to be Ordinary in that diocese.

*That those who dissent from, as well as those who assent to the ordination of women to the priesthood and episcopate are both loyal Anglicans.*

The second aspect to determining the way forward to legislation for admitting women to the episcopate of the Church of England is the question of what it means to declare 'that those who dissent from, as well as those who assent to the ordination of women to the priesthood and episcopate are both loyal Anglicans'. We submit that the discussion of Canon A4 above is of considerable importance in defining the parameters of what it means to be a loyal Anglican in the sense implied by the 1998 Lambeth Conference. We further believe that the Windsor process is currently making a useful contribution to the definition of the parameters of dissent from decisions made by due canonical process within a province of the Anglican Communion.

In 1978, the Lambeth Conference recognized that provinces of the Anglican Communion were free to ordain women to all stages of the threefold ministry when the time seemed right to each

---

Anglican or Lutheran bishops who are women visit England: they agree not to exercise an episcopal role in provinces which do not recognize their ordination. However, this is not a negation of the fact that they are legally, validly and legitimately ordained in their own church. Similarly, Katharine Jefferts Schori is a recognized member of the Primates' Meeting as Primate of TEC (USA), although some of the other Primates represent provinces of the Anglican Communion in which she could not be ordained deacon or priest, let alone bishop.

province.[8] The Lambeth Conference thus recognized the competence of each Province to make this decision. More specifically, the principle that the Church of England is competent to legislate on matters of order is enshrined in the 'A' canons and especially Canon A6. In these circumstances, we suggest that 'loyalty' to the Anglican Communion implies public recognition of and obedience to the decisions made by due canonical process by the province to which one belongs. Consequently, we contend that 'loyal Anglicans' are those who respect and abide by the decisions of the province to which they belong, whatever their private reservations.

This understanding of what it means to be a loyal Anglican helps to delineate the boundaries of dissent in the present discussion. As the Church of England considers how best to proceed to the admission of women to the episcopate, it is essential, as the Archbishop of Canterbury noted in an address to General Synod in July 2006, that the orders of the Church of England remain capable of being recognized as catholic orders in an ecumenical context.[9] We suggest that this means the character

---

8   Lambeth Conference 1978, resolution 21.

9   *Proceedings of General Synod* 37.2 (July 2006), pp. 33–4: 'We have claimed to be Catholic, to have a ministry that is capable of being universally recognized (even where in practice it does not have that recognition) because of its theological and institutional continuity. We have claimed to hold a faith that is not locally determined but shared through time and space with the fellowship of the baptized. We have claimed to celebrate sacraments that express the reality of a community which is more than the people present at any one moment with any one set of concerns. So at the very least we must recognize that Anglicanism as we have experienced it has never been just a loose grouping of people who care to describe themselves as Anglicans but enjoy unconfined local liberties. Argue for this if you will, but recognize that it represents something other than the tradition we have received and been nourished by in God's providence. ... Only if we can articulate some coherent core for this

and functions of the episcopal office must cohere with those outlined in ecumenical agreed statements such as the Porvoo statement, the ARCIC statements and more recently the work of the International Commission for Anglican–Orthodox Dialogue. As the Archbishop of Canterbury noted in the debate on women in the episcopate in July 2006,[10] in those statements the gender of the person ordained bishop has not been understood as touching on the essential character of the office. Therefore any arrangements made for those who dissent from the decision of the Church of England to allow women to become bishops, may not themselves undermine the nature of the episcopate as the Church of England has received it. The belief that the bishop, as ordinary, is the effective symbol of unity in the diocese is core to this. Any arrangement which has the intention or effect of creating a separate episcopal structure – and thereby essentially a separate succession – would undermine the jurisdiction of the Ordinary, and would undermine the overall catholic shape and ethos of the Anglican episcopate.

The Windsor Report is entirely clear that while pastoral arrangements for dissenting groups must be sufficient to provide a credible degree of security,[11] the idea of parallel jurisdictions is to be ruled out.[12] Indeed, it regards as 'axiomatic' the view that the functions, rights and responsibilities of bishops offering pastoral oversight to minority groups should be delegated from the diocesan bishop.[13] We contend that proposals for a third province, or for any other arrangements which seek to sidestep the ordinary jurisdiction of the diocesan bishop, do not abide by this principle. Such arrangements would create a church which was in all sacramental essentials a separate body, denying the validity of

---

tradition in present practice can we continue to engage plausibly in any kind of ecumenical endeavour, local as much as international.'

10   *Proceedings of General Synod* 37.2 (July 2006), pp. 97–8.
11   Windsor Report, §151.
12   Windsor Report, §154.
13   Windsor Report, §152.

many of the confirmations and ordinations performed within the church of which it was nominally a part.[14] As ordinations of women as bishops continued, and the number of those ordained deacon or priest by those bishops grew, it would become increasingly difficult to speak of recognition of orders within that church. The possibility of collegial episcopal leadership would diminish. The end result would be a nominally Anglican body in England which recognized the orders of some other episcopal churches, but not of the wider Church of England, or indeed of much of the Anglican Communion. It is difficult to see why such a body would wish to remain within the Anglican Communion at all.

### Living together as one Church

Previous reports have spoken of the need to balance charity and clarity[15] in making provision for the ordination of women to the episcopate while keeping within the Church those who are opposed. We have tried to make it clear that the catholicity of the Church cannot be maintained without setting some boundaries to disagreement. Within those boundaries, though, we believe that there must be the maximum possible provision for those who remain loyal to the Church of England but who nonetheless disagree with the decision of the majority: this is what it means to live in charity with one another.

This is not some kind of pragmatic bowing to the inevitable, but an essential part of living as Christ's body. One of the ways in which charity is lived out in the life of the Church is through allowing others to be different, even in ways that we believe to be wrong, and in recognizing that the other is also walking in the way of Christ, even if not in a way we can completely accept or even fully understand.

---

14  As the opening case-study makes clear, the Church of England already lives with a situation in which some believe that not every eucharistic celebration is valid.

15  Guildford Report, §37.

The principles of living together in charity are humility and recognition. Humility prevents the proponents of any view from claiming a monopoly on theological truth; it leads into the recognition that God may be at work in those with whom we disagree, and that they have a contribution to make to the whole. Both humility and recognition must be mutual if the body is to remain one.

The catholicity of the Church, then, is not shown most perfectly in uniformity. On the contrary, the Church is catholic precisely when it is able to embrace a variety of beliefs, so long as these cohere around the basic credal statements of the faith and common allegiance to the church's order. ARCIC has affirmed the diversity of catholicity:

> As God has created diversity among humans, so the Church's fidelity and identity require not uniformity of expression and formulation at all levels in all situations, but rather catholic diversity within the unity of communion. This richness of traditions is a vital resource for a reconciled humanity.[16]

A genuinely catholic church which includes within itself differences over the rightness of ordaining women will not seek to exclude those who disagree with that decision, but it must (for it cannot do otherwise) expect there to be acceptance of the decisions and actions of the Church, including mutual recognition of ordinations and the orders consequent on them. If those who disagree with a decision to ordain women are to be one Church with those who agree, then those of both views must accept the legitimacy, if not the rightness, of the decision that has been made.

An inclusively catholic position demands that, to the greatest possible extent, the minority be as respected and included in the

---

16   ARCIC, *The Gift of Authority*, §27.

life of the Church as the majority. In the case of the admission of women to the episcopate, it is clear that the ministry and morale of those who felt unable to accept the decision would be adversely affected if they were forced on a day-to-day basis to relate to bishops who were women. For pastoral reasons, it is therefore right that in such cases episcopal duties should be delegated. Nevertheless this needs to be done in such a way that the unity and coherence of the diocese are maintained at the level of overall policy and pastoral strategy, and without compromising the ordinary authority of the diocesan bishop on which the unity and coherence depend. It is this that the structure of Special Episcopal Arrangements (SEA), laid out below, is designed to enable. The arrangements we propose are substantially those we submitted to the Bishops of Guildford and Gloucester in May 2006. Further consideration of the issues that have been raised has reinforced our belief that proposals along these lines will enable the Church of England to give a practical shape to the principles of humility and mutual recognition which are called for by the General Synod motion of July 2006.

*Document 3*

## Appendix A: Underlying principles to the legislative proposal[17]

- *The Church of England is competent to make the decision to ordain women as bishops.* This principle is enshrined in the A canons and especially Canon A6. Further, the Lambeth Conference has given Provinces of the Anglican Communion permission to move on the question of the ordination of women to all stages of the threefold ministry when the time seems right to each province (Lambeth Conference 1978; Resolution 21).

- Legislation must express the Church's joyful acceptance of the decision to ordain women as bishops, whilst making suitable pastoral provision for those who continue to have difficulties with the ordained ministry of women.

- There may therefore be no discrimination in the enabling Measure. The historic and catholic identity of episcopal ministry and office must be retained, and women and men who

---

17   The principles presented in Appendix A and the proposals outlined in B below are a revised version of those included in the joint submission made by Affirming Catholicism and WATCH to the Bishops of Guildford and Gloucester (5 May 2006). They are included here with the permission of WATCH. In their present form, they are the responsibility of Affirming Catholicism alone. The members of the original drafting group were: (for WATCH): Canon Dr Susan Atkin (WATCH Executive Committee; member of General Synod); the Revd Mark Bennet (WATCH Executive Committee with responsibility for liaison with diocesan representatives); Christina Rees (Chair, National WATCH; member of General Synod and of Archbishops' Council); John Ward (solicitor; member of General Synod); (for Affirming Catholicism): the Revd Jonathan Clark (Chair of the working party; Rector of St Mary's Stoke Newington; Rector General of the Society of Catholic Priests); the Revd Richard Jenkins (Director, Affirming Catholicism); the Revd Dr Charlotte Methuen (Departmental Lecturer in Ecclesiastical History, Faculty of Theology, University of Oxford; member of the Faith and Order Advisory Group); the Revd Dr Barry Norris (Chair, Affirming Catholicism).

are appointed as bishop must have the same authority and
responsibilities.

- Pastoral provision for those who have private reservations
about the ordained ministry of women can – and should – be
made, but such provision may not create structures which
undermine the catholic order of the Church or suggest
ambivalence about the Church's decision to admit women to
the threefold ministry.
- If pastoral provision is to have the force of law, it must be
enshrined in secondary legislation or in an enforceable,
statutory code of practice.

In working out the extent of the pastoral provision, the following
fundamental principles should apply:

- There can be no amendment to Canon A4. That is, 'those who
are made, ordained or consecrated bishops priests or deacons'
according to the ordinal and by a Bishop of the Church of
England are 'to be accounted, both by themselves and others, to
be truly bishops, priests or deacons'.
- Consequently, there can be no re-ordination of a priest or
deacon ordained by a bishop of the Church of England who
subsequently moves to another diocese; similarly there can be
no re-confirmation.
- The pastoral provision may not create a parallel jurisdiction for
those who are not prepared to accept the ordained ministry of
women, but must seek the highest possible degree of
communion and the highest possible degree of permeability.
- Arrangements requiring those in favour of the ordination of
women to exercise sensitivity for those opposed in certain
pastoral circumstances must be balanced by reciprocal
arrangements for such circumstances requiring pastoral
sensitivity also from those who are opposed towards ordained
women and those who are in favour.

*Document 3*

With respect to dioceses and diocesan structures, the pastoral provisions must maintain the integrity of the diocese as the fundamental unit of the Church. In practice, this means that:

- The bishop is and must be recognised to be Ordinary in his/her diocese.
- Special bishops who exercise a ministry in a diocese where the Ordinary is a woman, or is male and not prepared to declare that he would not ordain women,[18] must therefore share in the ministry of the Ordinary.
- Special bishops must accordingly work within and according to the policies and practices of the diocese where they exercise their ministry.
- All bishops and all parishes of a diocese must continue to be part of the same synodical structures (through which *episope* is also exercised).

**Appendix B: Outline for possible legislation, associated regulations/code of practice and guidelines for good practice**

**I. MEASURE**

1. Repeal of the 1986 Deacons Measure,[19] both 1993 Priests Measures[20] and the Act of Synod.
2. General provision stating that it is lawful for all people to be ordained to the threefold ministry in accordance with provisions made by regulations and canon.[21] This puts women and men on an equal footing in the Measure.

---

18 This latter possibility depends on the terms of the regulations/code of practice. See Appendix B § III.1 below.
19 Deacons (Ordination of Women) Measure 1983. Pension provisions in that Measure might need to be transferred to the new one.
20 Priests (Ordination of Women) Measure ('the main 1993 Measure') and the Ordination of Women (Financial Provisions) Measures 1993.
21 See section 1 of the main 1993 Measure.

3. Enabling provision for Synod to amend canon to make provision for the ordination of all people to the threefold ministry.

4. Enabling provision for EITHER regulations OR a statutory code of practice to be made by Synod in relation to the exercise of episcopal authority.[22]

   In the latter case, all bishops should be obliged by the Measure to have regard to the code.

   In addition, provision should be made for alleged breaches of the regulations/code of practice to be referred to an independent body for mediation (in which the agreement of both parties would be binding) or arbitration (in which a decision would be imposed on both parties).[23]

   Provision should be made for establishing or defining that body.

5. Provision for the masculine to include the feminine in Canon, the BCP and the Ordinals.[24] This would happen automatically under the Interpretation Act 1978[25] for other legislation. This would avoid the need for unnecessary amendments and treats everyone equally.

---

22 For simplicity, we would suggest one or the other along with non-statutory guidelines for good practice (see § IV below). However, the House of Bishops may prefer to use both regulations and a statutory code, with different issues being allocated to each according to their importance.

23 Putting the detail of the arrangements for the exercise of episcopal authority in the code or into regulations keeps these discriminatory provisions out of primary legislation. The Measure can then be short and simple. This approach also gives Synod the necessary power to deal with this matter without reference to parliament. It would also put these provisions on a firmer legal footing than the existing Act of Synod given that the main 1993 Measure does not mention the Act.

24 Cf §§8 and 9 of the main 1993 Measure and Canon C4B.2 which would be revoked.

25 §§21–3, Interpretation Act 1978.

6.  The repeal of 1986 and 1993 Measures and Act of Synod and the commencement of provisions permitting ordinations of women bishops should not take place until the amendments to canon and the regulations/statutory code of practice have all been made as a package.[26]

## II. AMENDMENTS TO CANON

1.  Revocation of Canon C2.5 prohibiting the ordination of women to the episcopate.
2.  Revocation of Canons C4A.1 and C4B permitting the ordination of women to the diaconate and priesthood. These provisions would no longer be necessary because of provision made by the Measure. Canon C3 would apply to women and men.
3.  Revocation of remainder of Canon C4A (in relation to deaconesses and forms of service) as now unnecessary.
4.  Amendment of Canon C14 to allow oaths to be administered by a bishop exercising episcopal authority under the regulations/statutory code of practice and made to that bishop and the Ordinary.
5.  Extension of Canon C20 in relation to suffragans so that all bishops exercising episcopal authority under the regulations/statutory code of practice are under a duty to co-operate with the Ordinary who has assigned authority to them.

## III. REGULATIONS/CODE OF PRACTICE

1.  Provision for parishes to pass and withdraw resolutions in a Special Parochial Church Meeting in relation to women presidents and incumbents[27] and/or to pass and withdraw resolutions asking the Ordinary, if female, or if male and not

---

26  Cf. §12 of the main 1993 Measure.
27  Cf. sections 3 and 4 of the main 1993 Measure.

prepared to declare that he would not ordain women,[28] to exercise her/his authority in relation to a particular task or group of tasks through another bishop in the same or another diocese (Special Episcopal Arrangements [SEA]).

a) A *two-thirds* majority of a Special Parochial Church Meeting may pass one or more of the following resolutions:

I   That this parish would not accept a woman as the minister who presides or celebrates at Holy Communion or pronounces the absolution in the parish;

II   That this parish would not accept a woman as the incumbent of the parish;

III   That this parish requests that, in the event of a woman being appointed as bishop of the diocese, Special Episcopal Arrangements (SEA) be made.

IV   That this parish requests that, in the absence of any declaration by the bishop of the diocese for the time being that he would take part neither in the ordination of women priests nor the consecration of women bishops, arrangements for the sharing of episcopal ministry be made with a bishop who has made such declarations.[29]

b) Every member of the electoral roll must be given notice of and consulted about the resolutions before the meeting by means to be defined in the regulations/code of practice. In the event of a parish wishing to consider resolutions III or IV,

---

28   This latter provision pertains only if the option for resolution IV (see below) is included.

29   This resolution is based on the current Act of Synod. Affirming Catholicism believes that such a resolution would only be acceptable in conjunction with clear and enforceable provisions to ensure *both* a) proper care for women clergy and all those in favour of the ordination of women in those dioceses where the Ordinary is not prepared to ordain women to the priesthood and/or diaconate (see §III.4 below) *and* b) that the ministry of women as priests and bishops and of those in favour of the ordination of women was not restricted in any way by the extent of the role or jurisdiction of such a bishop except as explicitly permitted under the SEA proposals.

the Ordinary must meet with the Incumbent and Parochial Church Council before the SPCM.

c) An analogous procedure to enable the calling of an SPCM to consider the withdrawal of resolutions before the end of the five-year period, should the Parochial Church Council so advise.

d) Resolutions once passed to be reviewed at least every five years and at every vacancy, and to lapse after five years if not renewed.

e) Cathedrals and cathedral church parishes not to be authorised to pass any of these resolutions.

2. Provision setting out the Special Episcopal Arrangements under which an Ordinary may arrange for her authority to be exercised through a suffragan or area bishop in her diocese.

a) In parishes which had passed only resolutions I or II a woman Ordinary, while exercising all other episcopal functions, would respect the wishes of the parish and appoint a male substitute to exercise sacramental ministry. Special Episcopal Arrangements would be made only in the event of resolution III or IV being passed.[30]

b) Should a parish request Special Episcopal Arrangements, the Ordinary would be required to arrange the provision of ministry by another, male, bishop (henceforth referred to as the SEA bishop), authorizing him to exercise sacramental care and to share the pastoral and disciplinary functions of the Ordinary in respect of such parishes. The bishop so appointed would exercise a jurisdiction like that of an area bishop and would be a member of the senior staff of the diocese.[31]

---

30 This would allow parishes to continue to have the option of declining the sacramental ministry of women and/or preventing a woman from being licensed as incumbent of the parish, without automatically coming under the jurisdiction of a SEA bishop.

31 Cf. provisions under the Dioceses Measure 1978.

c) As area bishop, the SEA bishop would exercise sacramental ministry in the parish and would share pastoral care, ministerial review and disciplinary oversight of the clergy according to diocesan practice and policies.

d) The SEA bishop would act on behalf of the diocesan in relation to appointments by liaising with parishes in respect of vacancies and making recommendations for appointments to the Diocesan Bishop/Board of Patronage.

e) The SEA bishop would oversee the selection, training and ordination of such candidates for ministry as have requested his oversight, making recommendations to the diocesan about the sponsorship of specific candidates in accordance with diocesan practice and policies. Ordinands would be part of the national system of selection and training.

f) The SEA bishop would have power to initiate proposals in relation to pastoral measures within agreed diocesan strategies and policies and, as a member of the senior staff of the diocese, would have full voting rights in relation to parishes under his oversight and would be required to cooperate in any planning for mission and pastoral care.

g) Clergy in SEA parishes would make oaths to the SEA bishop as area bishop *and* to the diocesan. Oaths would be administered by the SEA bishop.[32]

3. Provision for the procedures to be followed with regard to SEA parishes in the event of the Ordinary's ceasing to be a

---

32 This is current practice in dioceses with an area system such as London where resolution 'C' parishes make oaths of canonical obedience to the Bishop of London and the Bishop of Fulham instead of their area bishop. London Plan, section 9: 'Any oaths to be taken to the Bishops of Stepney, Kensington, Willesden, Edmonton and Fulham at ordination to the priesthood, institution or licensings will also be taken to the Bishop of London as Ordinary'. See http://www.bishopoffulham.co.uk/Declaration.htm (last visited 28 March 2007).

woman or a man who is not prepared to declare that he would not ordain women.

4.  Provision setting out arrangements in the case when an Ordinary is not prepared to ordain women to the priesthood and/or diaconate.

    In the event that an Ordinary is not prepared to ordain women to the priesthood and/or the diaconate, he should be required to appoint an assistant bishop to assist him in the selection, training and ordination of women candidates for the ordained ministry, and their appointment, licensing and pastoral care. This assistant bishop should be a member of the senior staff of the diocese.

5.  Transitional provision for parishes or cathedrals which have passed the existing resolutions A, B or C, giving them sufficient time (to be defined, but probably less than one year) to consider the new resolutions.

## IV. GUIDELINES FOR GOOD PRACTICE

A number of matters must also be considered and non-statutory guidelines offered. These non-statutory guidelines would not be enforceable through arbitration but cases of dispute could be referred to mediation as described in I.4 above. It might therefore be preferred to deal with some of the questions raised below in the regulations/code of practice.

Matters to be dealt with in guidelines for good practice would include:

1.  An affirmation that where the whole Church acts, it should act according to the decisions it has made with respect to the ordination of women. For example, candidates and selectors at Bishops' Advisory Panels should expect that women priests who are selectors may preside at the eucharist.

2.  An explicit requirement that all those licensed to the Church of England, whatever their private reservations, should

recognize and teach that the Church of England does ordain women as deacons, priests and bishops.[33]

3. Arrangements for multi-parish benefices in which one parish or some but not all parishes have passed one or more of the resolutions.

4. Arrangements for schools, hospitals, prisons and other non-parochial institutions which exist within the boundaries of parishes which have passed any of resolutions I, II, III or IV.

5. Guidelines for appointments procedures, and in particular: a clear statement of how advertisements may or may not be phrased in the event that a parish has not passed resolution II (i.e. of how the provisions about advertising posts under the Sex Discrimination (Removal) Act affect the Church of England); a stated expectation that every candidate will make his or her position on the ordained ministry of women known during any appointment process; guidance about procedures to be followed when an appointment involves a patron other than the diocesan bishop or diocesan patronage board; guidance about procedures to be followed in non-parochial appointments; particular rules allowing the diocese in Europe to place gender-specific advertisements for posts in places where local ecumenical circumstances make this necessary, and guidelines for determining when this is the case. (This may have to be in the regulations/statutory code of practice since it involves a dispensation from the Sex Discrimination (Removal) Act.)

6. Guidelines governing the appointment, role and responsibilities of diocesan deans for women's ministry.

7. Pastoral provision to be made for those not prepared to accept the ordained ministry of women in particular circumstances, along the lines of the current legislation. Thus, couples, baptismal candidates or their parents and those bereaved may request a male officiant at appropriate pastoral offices in

---

33 A statement to this effect could be added to the preamble of the Declaration of Assent.

churches where there is a woman incumbent or to which a woman is licensed; similarly candidates for priesting may request that women priests not lay on hands at the ordination.

These provisions to become reciprocal: couples, baptismal candidates or their parents or those bereaved may request a particular woman officiant at pastoral offices in parishes which have passed any of the resolutions; no priest present at an ordination shall be prevented from laying hands on any candidate except one who has specifically requested otherwise.

## Appendix C: A juridical consideration of Canon A4

Introductory remarks

> Canon A4 has not been abrogated; there are no plans to abrogate it; and indeed since it is part of the law of the land, this Synod alone has no power to abrogate it.[34]

The motion approving the setting-up of this legislative drafting group was successfully amended in General Synod to include the phrase 'consistent with Canon A4'. The debate on this amendment showed that the motivation for its insertion was to ensure that whatever provision was made for those opposed to the ordination of women to the episcopate, all lawfully conferred orders of ministers in the Church of England should be recognized as such by all.

### The conclusions of Forward in Faith

The legal working party of Forward in Faith has submitted a contribution to the Women Bishops Legislative Drafting Group.[35] The Forward in Faith working party concludes that the addition

---

34  The Archbishop of Canterbury, *Proceedings of General Synod* (July 2006), Vol. 37, no. 2, p. 294.

35  See http://www.forwardinfaith.com/news/pages/Consistent_with_Canon_A4.pdf

of the words 'consistent with Canon A4' add nothing to the original motion. In coming to this conclusion the working party makes the following points *inter alia*:

a. That the decision to ordain women to the priesthood was in some sense 'provisional', that that decision is in the process of being received and that it could be reversed [§§5–6].

b. That included in the decision to ordain women to the priesthood was permission to hold in question of the validity of these ordinations [§§5–7].

c. That the Eames Commission Report in 1990 and the Rochester Report in 2004 are mistaken when they say that whilst the decision to ordain women to the priesthood is open to reversal, the orders of those women ordained are not open to question [§§ 9–10].

d. That resolutions A and B of the Priests (Ordination of Women) Measure 1993 can be interpreted as allowing members of the Church of England to reject the validity of the orders of women priests [§11].

e. That Canon A4 only refers to ordinations carried out according to the rite of the Ordinal attached to the *Book of Common Prayer* [§12].

f. That Canon A4 does not require anyone to assent to anybody's orders [§12].

g. That even if it does, then it has been abrogated or suspended by the contrary provisions of the 1993 Measure and its resolutions A and B [§15].

*Validity and lawfulness*

A key premise of the working party's paper is that the Church of England maintains a doctrine of validity of ordination similar to that of the Roman Catholic Church. Roman Catholic sacramental theology and canon law sets down certain conditions for valid ordination. If these conditions are not fulfilled then the ordination is not valid and consequently inoperative, as are any sacramental functions performed by the invalidly ordained person. The terms valid and invalid are nowhere found in the canons, liturgical texts and historic formularies that form part of the canon law of the Church of England.[36] Instead the Church of England has historically set great store by the lawfulness of ordination. Canon A4 stands in a long line of canons, articles and rubrics which, when viewed together, can be seen to conclude as follows:

a. Episcopal ordination is necessary before a person can function lawfully as a bishop, priest or deacon in the Church of England.[37] This requirement caused ministers not episcopally ordained to be expelled from their benefices in 1662. At the time of the reformation the threefold order of ministry and the bishop as the invariable minister of ordination continued.

b. The Church of England's ordination liturgy, in this case the ordinal of 1662, is sufficient for ordaining candidates to the three orders of ministry.

c. Individuals are not at liberty to hold that ordination according to the Ordinal is unlawful or insufficient.

English law's silence on validity of orders contrasts with what it says about validity of marriage. A marriage can be valid and consequently effective or invalid and consequently null. A person domiciled in England who marries someone abroad whilst one party is below the legal age for marriage in this country is not considered to be validly married.[38] In contrast, English women ordained abroad prior to 1994 were not considered to have invalid orders. Once ordination of women to the priesthood became possible in the Church of England they were capable of taking up that ministry without re-ordination. It is not that English canon

---

36 See generally Will Adam, 'The Reception, Recognition and Reconciliation of Holy Orders' in *Ecclesiastical Law Journal* 4 (2005), p. 7

37 Act of Uniformity 1662 s. 10.

38 *Pugh v Pugh* [1951] 2 All ER 680.

law has nothing to say about validity, it is just that it has consistently refused to apply concepts of validity to ordination.

## The principle of acceptance enshrined in Canon A4

The requirement of the acceptance by all of the orders of lawfully ordained ministers of the Church of England has a long and distinguished history. Even though Canon A4 is (arguably) not primary legislation, it mirrors the rubrics of the ordinal and Article 36 of the Thirty-Nine Articles, both of which documents have primary statutory force. It is certainly arguable that Article 36 and Canon A4 refer only to the ordinal annexed to the *Book of Common Prayer* and not to authorised alternative services of ordination. However, it can equally be argued that underlying the provisions of Canon A4 is a specific and constantly applied principle that those lawfully ordained are lawfully ordained and should be accepted as such.

Canon A4 states the following:

    i.   The ordinal is not repugnant to the Word of God;
   ii.   Those ordained according to it are lawfully ordained;
  iii.   They ought to be accounted as truly bishops, priests or deacons by themselves and others.

Canon 8 of 1603/4 has largely the same wording but rather than being a statement of the *fact* of the lawfulness and truth of Anglican ordination it is worded as a warning that anyone who says otherwise, or who suggests that 'some other calling' (in Latin *alium ordinationem*) is necessary, is to be excommunicated *ipso facto* and not restored without repentance and public revocation of 'such his wicked errors'.

Canon 6§2 of the 1571 draft is the nearest relation in earlier draft canons. It states that the 'book of common prayers [*sic*] and the book of the consecration of archbishops, bishops, ministers and deacons contain nothing repugnant to' the doctrine of the Church (in this canon this doctrine is described as being set out in the scriptures and articles). Article 36 of 1562/71 states that all ordained since the second year of Edward VI (i.e. according to the ordinal) 'we declare all such to be rightly, orderly, and lawfully consecrated and ordered'. This article remains as Article 36.

The preface to the Ordinal, first published in 1549, soon after the first Book of Common Prayer, remained unchanged through the revisions to the ordinal of 1552 and was incorporated as the Preface to the Ordinal in the Book of Common Prayer 1662. It states that the orders conferred therewith should be 'esteemed'.

### *'Ought to be accounted'*

The Forward in Faith working party understands the term 'ought' to be not binding, but aspirational. However, 'ought' is not to be considered a weak word. Elsewhere in the Canons it is stated that the church *ought* to observe certain fasts[39] and that husband and wife *ought* to help and comfort each other.[40] These instructions are not merely aspirational. Through them, the Church of England states with the power of law that fasts are to be observed, that spouses are to be mutually supportive – and that lawful orders should be recognized. Allegiance to the Church demands that its members should do all in their power to conform themselves in thought, word and deed to the Church's teaching. Individuals are not at liberty to hold contrary positions.

### *Resolutions A and B*

Resolutions A and B formed part of the Priests (Ordination of Women) Measure 1993. They allowed a PCC (not an individual) to prevent a woman priest from (a) presiding at the eucharist and/or (b) being appointed as an incumbent of that parish. The assertion that these resolutions encourage or permit refusal to recognize the lawfulness (or the validity) of women's orders needs to be challenged.

---

39   Canon B6.4.
40   Canon B30.1.

It has been demonstrated above that the Church of England does not, and never has, held to a concept of validity when it comes to ordination, rather it concentrates on lawfulness. It has also been demonstrated that the principle enshrined in Canon A4 is as old as the Church of England itself. Legislation to enable clergy ordained overseas to minister in the Church of England was founded on the principle that recognizably Anglican ordination is accepted as lawful and is not repeated. Whilst it was not lawful for women to be ordained as priests in the Church of England women priests ordained in other parts of the Anglican Communion were not permitted to function as priests but their orders were not held to be 'invalid' as evidenced by the fact that they did not need to be ordained again after the 1993 measure came into force.

There is a clear thread of argument in the Forward in Faith working party's submission that the Church of England accepts that individual Anglicans may legitimately reject the orders of certain deacons, priests and bishops of the Church of England. Furthermore, the Report points to resolutions A and B in support of this view. This argument is not sustainable.

Recognition of lawful ordination has never been within the competence of an individual or of a PCC. Canon A4 makes this clear. Those who are lawfully ordained and licensed or permitted to officiate by the bishop[41] or archbishop are capable of ministry.

Resolutions A and B do not indicate that it is possible for individuals or groups to disregard the principle of Canon A4, although they have undoubtedly been used in this way. All that resolutions A and B do is in some way to fetter the discretion of certain people in the way they exercise their legal powers. Resolution A fetters the discretion, for instance, of an incumbent (or of sequestrators in a vacancy) as to whom they can invite to celebrate the eucharist in the parish church.[42] Resolution B fetters

---

41 Or temporarily by an incumbent with certain conditions – Canon C8.
42 Powers under Canon C8.

*Document 3*

the discretion of the patron, bishop and parish representatives in the appointment of an incumbent.[43] It is important to note that it is the PCC who must make this decision – it is not about private acceptance or rejection of orders by individuals – and that PCCs do not need to give a reason for their decision. Reasons for passing the resolutions vary. A PCC could pass resolution A, for instance, simply because a majority of them do not like the sound of a woman's voice singing the preface to the eucharistic prayer. Resolution B was passed in the mid 1990s by PCCs that believed that no female candidate would, at the time, have had sufficient experience to do the job in hand. Evangelical views that women *should not* be in a position of leadership are not necessarily analogous to the view that they *cannot* be ordained as priests or bishops.

Recognition is the function of the bishop or archbishop, not of an individual and even then, only according to law rather than private judgment. Bishops must recognize the orders of all those who are considered lawfully ordained according to the law of the Church of England. However, a bishop is not bound at all times and in all places to permit every person whose orders he recognizes to perform the function of their ministry. There are systems of appointment, licensing and permission, which need to be gone through prior to an individual ministering. This process does not indicate at any point that the orders of an individual are open to question or that sacraments and other functions performed by them are consequently inoperative. A bishop, priest or deacon coming from overseas needs a licence from the Archbishops under the Overseas Clergy Measure. Once that licence has been granted it is not up to other individual bishops or any other person to cast doubt on that person's orders, but they do not have to permit them to function in their diocese and an incumbent does not need to invite them to minister.

---

43   Powers under the Patronage (Benefices) Measure 1986.

*Final remarks*

The argument offered by the Forward in Faith working party, that the existence of the resolutions and of the Episcopal Ministry Act of Synod implies that observance of Canon A4 has been suspended, cannot be sustained. These different pieces of legislation are entirely consistent with one another. The canon was not amended by the 1993 Measure. The authentic Church of England position is that whilst Canon A4 might strictly only apply to ordinations according to the 1662 ordinal, the principle enshrined in it is part of Anglican self-understanding.[44] It is not up to individuals or groups to cast doubt on the authenticity of the orders of lawfully ordained ministers. Resolutions A and B can be seen as fettering discretion in the processes for appointing, licensing and inviting priests to perform certain functions and fill certain posts. If resolutions A and B are consistent with Canon A4 (which they must be as the measure did not amend the canon) then they did not give anybody authority to hold a view contrary to that canon and to the relevant article.

The Episcopal Ministry Act of Synod should also be read as consistent with Canon A4. It allows diocesan bishops to invite suffragan bishops of the dioceses of Canterbury and York to fulfil certain functions within their dioceses. That is, it is about appointing, licensing and permitting proper persons to carry out those functions and is entirely consistent with Canon A4 and Article 36. It is not about recognizing or not recognizing orders.

The same principles will apply to the orders of female bishops. No bishop will be forced to nominate a woman as a suffragan bishop. However, a woman who is a bishop will have been ordained lawfully and it would be a departure from the Anglican tradition to allow individuals or groups to cast doubt on her orders or on the efficacy of functions performed by her. This latter point is very important. Ministerial functions – particularly those

---

44 By this token, women ordained according to the 1662 ordinal would in any case fall under Canon A4.

of bishops – can and do affect the legal status of a person and to cast doubt on the legal status of some individuals could lead to great confusion. For instance, presiding at a legally recognizable marriage in the Church of England requires one to be in holy orders; a Church of England marriage conducted by someone not in holy orders would be open to question and may be voidable. The logic of not recognizing the orders of a woman bishop is that one does not recognize the orders of those ordained by her. This in turn raises questions about the recognition of the functions performed by those persons and consequently about the legal status of those to whom those persons minister, for instance in marriage.

To introduce an option of non-recognition of validity of certain ministers' orders would be to introduce an unwelcome and confusing novelty far greater than the novelty of women bishops.

### Appendix D: A historical note on the provenance of Canon A4

A4: *Of the Form and Manner of Making, Ordaining, and Consecrating of Bishops, Priests, and Deacons*
The Form and Manner of Making, Ordaining, and Consecrating of Bishops, Priests, and Deacons, annexed to The Book of Common Prayer and commonly known as the Ordinal, is not repugnant to the Word of God; and those who are so made, ordained, or consecrated bishops, priests, or deacons, according to the said Ordinal, are lawfully made, ordained, or consecrated, and ought to be accounted, both by themselves and others, to be truly bishops, priests, or deacons.

Canon A4 in its present form first appeared as Canon 4 in the proposed canons of 1947, in the first section 'The Church of England', which in the 1964 canons became the A canons. Like the other A canons, Canon A4 has its origins in the 1603/4 canons. These canons, 'the most serious attempt the post-reformation church [of England] ever made to reduce its canon law to order',[45] were drafted on the accession of King James VI of Scotland as James I of England, in part as an attempt to reconcile the Puritans and the establishment.[46] These canons were the first to be declared not to lapse on the death of the sovereign.[47] The canons were approved by the Convocation of Canterbury in June 1604[48] and by the Convocation of York in March 1606.[49] Convocation approved the Latin text, which therefore became authoritative, although the English text was prior and frequently cited.[50]

The opening section of the 1603/4 canons underlines the constitutional character of the Church of England. The canons in this section deal with royal supremacy, the articles of religion, the *Book of Common Prayer*, and ministry. The headings of these canons demonstrate that they are intended primarily to establish the legality and the lawfulness of the Church of England's existence and its establishment, as can be seen from their headings:[51]

1. The King's supremacy over the Church of England in causes ecclesiastical to be maintained.
2. Impugners of the King's supremacy censured.
3. The Church of England a true and apostolical church.

---

45 Gerald Bray (ed.) *The Anglican Canons 1529–1947*, Church of England Record Society 6 (Woodbridge: Boydell, 1998), p. 258, note 2.
46 Bray, *Anglican Canons*, p. liv–lv.
47 Bray, *Anglican Canons*, p. lv, n. 76.
48 Bray, *Anglican Canons*, p. lvi.
49 Bray, *Anglican Canons*, p. lix.
50 Bray, *Anglican Canons*, p. lix.
51 Bray, *Anglican Canons*, pp. 262-81. Where the headings are given in English only, the Latin and the English correspond. Where they differ, the Latin is given in italics, followed by an English translation also in italics.

*Ecclesia Anglicana orthodoxa. [The Church of England an orthodox church].*

4. Impugners of the public worship of God established in the Church of England, censured.
*Divina cultus ratio in ecclesia Anglicana stabilita, pia et orthodoxa. [The order of divine service established in the Church of England pious and orthodox].*

5. Impugners of the articles of religion established in the Church or England, censured.
*Doctrinae articuli in ecclesia Anglicana stabiliti, pii et orthodoxi. [The articles of teaching established in the Church of England pious and orthodox].*

6. Impugners of the rites and ceremonies established in the Church of England, censured.
*Ceremoniarum in ecclesia Anglicana obtinentium usus, pius et licitus. [The ceremonies generally used in the Church of England pious and lawful].*

7. Impugners of the government of the Church of England by archbishops, bishops, etc. censured.
*Ecclesiae Anglicanae administratio verbo divini consona. [The administration of the Church of England consonant with the divine word].*

8. Impugners of the form of consecrating and ordering archbishops, bishops, etc. in the Church of England, censured.
*Cleri ordinandi ratio in ecclesia Anglicana verbo divino consona. [The order of ordaining clergy in the Church of England consonant with the divine word].*

9. Authors of schism in the Church of England censured.

10. Maintainers of schismatics in the Church of England censured.

11. Maintainers of conventicles censured.

12. Maintainers of constitutions made in conventicles censured.

It is noticeable that where the Latin departs from the English, it is replaces a condemnation with a positive statement. Thus the heading of the English text of Canon 8 focuses on those who dissent from the practice of the Church of England – 'Impugners of the form of consecrating and ordering archbishops, bishops, etc. in the Church of England, censured' – whilst the Latin form declares the ordinal to be 'consonant with the word of God'. The earlier, English, text appears to define and condemn those who condemn the Church of England, whilst the Latin text expresses the authors' confidence that the Church of England exists as a church consonant with God's word, with right teaching, proper administration of the sacraments through its liturgy, and a legitimately ordered ministry. This first section of the 1603/4 canons is intended to establish the Church of England as the catholic Church in England.

The body of Canon 8 demonstrates that its affirmation of the orthodoxy of the ordinal has deeper implications. This is an affirmation that those ordained bishop, priest or deacon in the Church of England are indeed bishops, priests and deacons and that nobody, on pain of excommunication, is to account them otherwise. Translated into English, the Latin version of Canon 8 reads:

> The order of ordaining clergy in the Church of England is consonant with the word of God:
> Anyone who affirms or teaches, that the form and rite of ordaining or inaugurating bishops, priests and deacons contains anything within it which is repugnant to the word of God, and that those who by this means have ever been made bishops priests or deacons are not rightly ordained or cannot be held by themselves or by any other to be bishops priests or deacons until they have been ordained by another rite, is excommunicated by that fact

and can never be absolved until he has repented and has publicly recanted his impious errors.[52]

The contemporary English version of Canon 8 reads:

> *Impugners of the Form of consecrating and ordering Archbishops, Bishops, &c., in the Church of England, censured*: Whoever shall hereafter affirm or teach, that the form and manner of making and consecrating Bishops, Priests, and Deacons, containeth anything in it that is repugnant to the Word of God, or that they who are made Bishops, Priests, or Deacons, in that form, are not lawfully made, nor ought to be accounted, either by themselves or others, to be truly either Bishops, Priests or Deacons, until they have some other calling to those divine offices; let him be excommunicated *ipso facto,* not to be restored until he repent, and publicly revoke such his wicked errors.[53]

The link between the validity of the rite of ordination – 'the form and manner of making, ordaining and consecrating bishops, priests and deacons' – and the validity of the orders, implicit in the modern Canon A4, is explicitly stated in the 1603/4 Canon 8, not least in the statement in the Latin text that it is unacceptable on pain of excommunication to refuse to recognize the orders of those ordained in the Church of England 'until they have been ordained by another rite'. What is at stake here is not a sense of vocation ('another calling'), but the affirmation that the Church of England's ordinal is capable of making 'real' bishops, priests and deacons. The canon thus reflects the traditional catholic understanding that a person is lawfully ordained only if they are a

52 Bray, *Anglican Canons*, pp. 274, 276.
53 Bray, *Anglican Canons*, pp. 275, 277.

legitimate candidate who has been ordained by a correct and authorized rite.[54]

It is apparent that the modern Canon A4 derives from this Canon, reworded to take the form of a positive statement. Given that the intention of the modern 'A' canons is, like the first group of the 1603/4 canons, to establish the legitimacy of the Church of England and its competence to define and order its life, it is scarcely surprising that it includes an affirmation of the orders of that church.

## Appendix E: Members of the working party

The Revd Will Adam (Priest in Charge of Girton; Ely Diocesan Ecumenical Officer); the Revd Dr Mark Chapman (Vice-Principal, Ripon College, Cuddesdon); the Revd Jonathan Clark (Chair of the working party; Rector of St Mary's Stoke Newington; Rector General of the Society of Catholic Priests; member of the steering group for Affirming Catholicism in General Synod); the Revd Richard Jenkins (Director, Affirming Catholicism); the Revd Dr Charlotte Methuen (Departmental Lecturer in Ecclesiastical History, University of Oxford; Canon Theologian of Gloucester Cathedral).

---

54  See note 4 above.

**Document 4: Affirming Catholicism: Letter to the Bishop of Manchester from the Revd Jonathan Clark with some clarifications after meeting with the Women Bishops' Legislative Drafting Group (7 September 2007)**

*Women Bishops' Legislative Drafting Group: clarifications*

During our presentation to the General Synod Women Bishop's Legislative Drafting Group, the members of the Affirming Catholicism group were impressed by the candour and openness with which we were received and felt that we received a thorough hearing. It seemed to us to that there were two related areas where further clarification of our position might be helpful: first, over the importance of seeing episcopacy in relation to the wider representative structures of synodality; and second, over what appears to be one of the major problems for those opposed to the ordination of women as bishops – the nature of the 'ordinary jurisdiction' of the bishop, and the oath of canonical obedience to somebody concerning whose orders they have doubts. Although these clarifications are offered by the Affirming Catholicism working group as a whole, we are particularly indebted to Dr Mark Chapman for his substantial contribution to our thinking.

*Ordinary jurisdiction, synodality and mission*

1. The principal theological underpinning of our submission rests in our understanding of the unity and the catholicity of the Church, and their expression in the life of the diocese. The Church of England has inherited a structure of parishes and dioceses which cover every square inch of the country. The unity and catholicity of the Church are expressed in part through this territorial principle – each parish in turns belongs to a deanery and to a diocese. The diocese, deanery, and parish structures together symbolize the unity of the Church at a local level. All people who are resident in parishes can become members of electoral rolls and can participate in the life of the Church through the structures of the parish, the deanery, the diocese, and the General Synod which

give expression to the Church's catholicity. This representative structure works in dialogue with the leadership of the Church exercised through its bishops and clergy. Although some parish churches have developed a culture defined by a particular tradition, including some parishes which have petitioned for pastoral and sacramental ministry from a PEV, at present no parish can opt out of diocesan structures without ceasing to belong to the Church of England. Anything that threatens this fundamental principle by creating any kind of parallel jurisdiction would lead to a breakdown of the participative structures of the Church and consequently the common life of the people of God. While the synodical structures of the Church of England might be said to have developed in a piecemeal and unplanned way, they nonetheless express the common life of the Church of England and bind its people together in a body defined by catholicity rather than congregationalism or parochialism.

2. Pragmatically, a unified decision-making structure makes strategic pastoral planning possible, as well as ensuring the most efficient use and deployment of scarce resources. More importantly, however, it best serves the mission of God throughout the Church. A unified church with one set of canons expresses the ability of Christians to live together in unity despite significant levels of disagreement, and guarantees to all people that wherever they might live they can become members of the Church of England. To give the right of choice of jurisdiction to a particular parish is to adopt a congregationalist church polity in which authority and oversight are exercised primarily at the level of the congregation.

3. Legally (i.e. 'canonically') the unity of the diocese is expressed through the jurisdiction that is attached to a particular ecclesiastical office ('ordinary jurisdiction'). Within the inherited structures of the Church of England the superior ordinary jurisdiction in a diocese has been exercised by the diocesan bishop, although certain matters (particularly connected with visitations) fall within the ordinary jurisdiction of the archdeacon

---

Document 4

(of which there are now a significant number who are women). At a parish level, every incumbent or equivalent is 'ordinary' in his or her benefice, but subject to his or her superior ordinary (usually the bishop, but also other clergy including team rectors). The unity of the Church is expressed through one bishop in one territorial diocese who is the superior ordinary, but who delegates certain functions to other people, most obviously area bishops.

4. Traditionally, ordinary jurisdiction has extended over teaching, governing, adjudicating, and administering the sacraments, although every ordinary has the right to delegate jurisdiction within the territorial limits of his (or her) jurisdiction, subject to legal provisions. This means that the bishop remains 'superior' ordinary of the diocese even in those places where he has delegated his sacramental and pastoral roles to another bishop. Most importantly, he is still responsible for ensuring that the canons of the Church are obeyed and due process is followed in ecclesiastical affairs.[1] It would be difficult to envisage a situation where there could be two superior ordinaries in one and the same territory and for the Church of England to remain one church.

5. It has been suggested that the current situation in which there are overlapping jurisdictions in continental Europe, both of dioceses of the Anglican Communion and of other churches with which we are in full communion, provides legitimacy for independent dioceses with their own ordinary jurisdiction, overlaid on the present structure of geographical dioceses.[2] This argument, we believe, ignores the crucial fact that the situation in Europe has been recognized by successive Lambeth Conferences to be anomalous and unfortunate, arising out of a variety of

---

1   The importance of the oath of canonical obedience and the corresponding legal obligations which need to be exercised by the ordinary were stressed in the judgement to the *Coekin v Bishop of Southwark* Appeal to Archbishop of Canterbury (June 2006). See *Ecclesiastical Law Journal* 9 (2007), pp. 145–7.

2   Bishop Andrew Burnham, 'How Can Brazil Help?', in *New Directions* (July 2007), p. 4.

192

chaplaincy and mission initiatives, and considerable energy has been expended on attempting to integrate the various jurisdictions. To make this much-criticized structure a pattern for future provision for those opposed to the ordination of women therefore seems very odd. Moreover, the General Synod has in the last year expended significant time and effort in ensuring that 'fresh expressions of Church' are integrated into diocesan structures and are in relation to their bishop. This cannot be a key factor in the life of the Church at one moment, and a dispensable extra the next.

6. In order to ensure the coherence and common life of the diocese superior ordinary jurisdiction needs to continue to be exercised by the diocesan bishop (male or female), who oversees the structures of the diocese, as well as ensuring that canon law is obeyed by all those exercising ecclesiastical functions. In the case where some bishops are women, clearly defined areas will need to be delineated in the proposals in order to take account of the theological position of those opposed to the ordination of women bishops. These needs can be respected by ensuring that the canonical or legal (rather than sacramental) aspect of the canons is stressed.

*Oaths of canonical obedience*

7. The earliest form of oath was obedience to the sacred canons of the Church, which were gradually identified with the person responsible for their administration. The oath of canonical obedience was thus not primarily one of personal or of unlimited obedience but of obedience to the administrator of the canons. The purpose of the oath was that the general discipline and canons of the Church were obeyed. This means that the person to whom the oath is made is the lawful and duly appointed administrator of the canons. This was very carefully circumscribed long ago in the case of *Long v. The Bishop of Cape Town*:

The Oath of Canonical Obedience does not mean that the clergyman will obey all such commands as the bishop makes against which there is no law, but that he will obey all such commands as the bishop by law is authorised to impose.[3]

This sense of obedience was held to be what was meant by the qualification 'canonical'. This legal aspect is emphasized by the fact that in certain cases, such as that of clergy serving in Royal Peculiars, the oath is not made to a bishop – or even to an ordained person at all – but to a person who has 'ordinary' legal (but not sacramental) jurisdiction. This is implied in the oath made by the canons of Westminster Abbey which recognizes the supremacy of the Queen (a laywoman) in all things.[4]

8. Our proposal is consequently that oaths of canonical obedience should be made by all licensed clergy (and others who hold ecclesiastical office) to the diocesan bishop, whether a man or woman, and whatever the views about the ordination of women bishops of the clergyman or woman being asked to make the oath, recognizing the precise limits and the legal nature of their jurisdiction. In other words, the ordinary jurisdiction of the diocese would be maintained through the traditional pattern of episcopal and archidiaconal oversight, but would apply only to those matters reserved for such jurisdiction. These would focus on

---

3   G. C. Brodrick and W. H. Fremantle, *Ecclesiastical Judgments of the Privy Council* (London: John Murray, 1865), p. 313.

4   The English translation of the Latin oath is as follows: 'I, *NN*, calling God to witness, promise and vow that I will embrace the true religion of Christ with my whole heart, that I will set the authority of scripture before the judgments of men, that I will seek the rule of life, and the whole of faith, from the word of God, and all other things which are not proved by the word of God I will hold to be merely human. That I will hold the authority of The Queen to be supreme in all things and I will oppose with my whole will and mind opinions contrary to the word of God. That in the cause of religion I will prefer truth to custom, written law to unwritten law.'

participation in the diocesan structures (including due process in election and appointment to diocesan bodies), as well as the proper administration of the law.

9. Although a desirable corollary of ordinary jurisdiction would be that the episcopal ordinary of the diocese would also act as the 'superior' sacramental minister to symbolize and manifest the unity of the Church in the diocese, this is not a necessary aspect of ordinary jurisdiction. All sacramental and pastoral roles of the bishop could be delegated by the ordinary to other suitable persons, if necessary through the force of canon. Our suggestion in the proposals presented to the Bishops of Gloucester and Guildford was that an oath would be made to both the Ordinary of the diocese as chief administrator of canons, as well as to the particular bishop who had been delegated by that Ordinary to perform sacramental and pastoral roles. Such bishops would share in the formal structure of the diocese as assistant bishops with a clearly designated set of roles and powers. They would play their part in pastoral oversight of the whole diocese through membership of the senior diocesan leadership, thus maintaining and expressing the unity and catholicity of the local church.

# Index

Act of Synod 9, 105–6
Alexander, Michael
  Solomon 96
Anglican–Methodist
  Covenant 45, 47, 50
Anglo-Catholicism 92–101
*Apostolicae Curae* 113
Aquinas 17
ARCIC 14–15, 65, 114, 164

*Baptism, Eucharist, Ministry*
  53–4
Baum, Gregory 106
Bultitude, Elizabeth 49
Burrus, Virginia 88

*Call for Women Bishops* 1, 6–7
Canon A4 184–9
Canons 1603/4 26, 180–1
*Catechism of the Catholic
  Church* 33
Chrysostom, John 76, 91
Congar, Yves 147
*Consecrated Women?* 1, 77–8
Cyprian 112

Dalferth, Ingolf 102
Daniélou, Jean 74
*Didascalia Apostolorum* 83, 85
Dixon, Jane Holmes 13
*Dominus Iesus* 113

Elizabeth I 23

Epiphanius 89
*Episcopal Ministry* 94, 107
*episkope* 69

Fairbairn, A. M. 105
Firmilian of Caesarea 83, 84
Forward in Faith 176–7

Geertz, Clifford 37
Gladstone, W. E. 98–9
Gobat, Samuel 99
Greeley, Andrew 39
Guildford report 10, 11, 105,
  108

Harris, Barbara 10
Harris, Harriet 6, 12
Harrison, Benjamin 99–100
Henry VIII 21
Hill, Mike 60
Hoare, Rupert 57
Hooker, Richard 26–7
Huber, Johannes 67
Hugh of St Victor 121–2
Hughes, Hugh Price 51
Hünermann, Peter 34

Ignatius
  *epistle to the Magnesians* 81
  *epistle to the Trallians* 81
Irish, Carolyn Tanner 6

Jerome 77

197

*Index*

Jerusalem Bishopric 4, 29,
95–101
Jewel, John 25–6
Johannesdotter, Jürgen 150
Jones, Ian 8, 108

Kasper, Walter 110–23,
126–7
Keble, John 95
*King's Book* 23
Küry, Urs 62

Laud, William 103
*Long v. The Bishop of Cape
Town* 193–4

Makhulu, Walter 7
Mary Magdalen 119
McCulloch, Nigel 129
Methodism 10, 43–61
and episcopacy 50–9
*Ministry in the Church* 15
*Mulieris Dignitatem* 39–40

Newman, J. H. 14, 92–3,
101
Nikolaou ,Theodor 70
Nockles, Peter 100

Oakeley, Frederick 96
Oaths of Canonical
Obedience 193–5
Old Catholic Churches 62–
71
Ordinary jurisdiction 190–
93

*Ordinatio Sacerdotalis* 33, 35
Origen 77, 82

Palmer, William 96
Perham, Michael 126
Philo 82
Porvoo Churches 10, 43
Pusey, E. B. 97–9

Rashdall, Hastings 1
Reininger, Dorothea 35
Reinkens, Joseph Hubert 64
Resolutions A and B 181–2
Rochester Report 10, 11,
108, 124
Russell, Norman 125

*Saepius Officio* 113
Sedgwick, Jonathan 4
Sharp, John 27–8
synodality 66–71

Tavard, George 48
Thirty-nine Articles 22, 24–
5, 95
Tillard, Jean-Marie 56
Tours, Council of 86–8
Tracy, David 38
Transferred Episcopal
Arrangements (TEA) 9,
109, 125
Trent, Council of 31–2

United Methodist Church
43-4
Utrecht, Union of 70

198

# Biblical References